TO

_____

FROM

_____

DATE

_____

A Prayer a Day for Mothers

Copyright © 2020 by DaySpring. All Rights Reserved.

First Edition, March 2020

Published by:

21154 Highway 16 East
Siloam Springs, AR 72761
dayspring.com

Unless otherwise noted, Scripture is taken from the Christian Standard Bible. Copyright © 2017 by Holman Bible Publishers. Used by permission. Christian Standard Bible®, and CSB® are federally registered trademarks of Holman Bible Publishers, all rights reserved.

Scripture quotations marked HCSB are taken from the Holman Christian Standard Bible®. Copyright © 1999, 2000, 2002, 2003, 2009 by Holman Bible Publishers. Used by permission. HCSB® is a federally registered trademark of Holman Bible Publishers.

Scripture quotations marked AMP are taken from the Amplified® Bible, © 1954, 1958, 1962, 1964, 1965, 1987 by The Lockman Foundation. Used by permission. (www.lockman.org)

Scripture quotations marked TLB are taken from The Living Bible with permission from Tyndale House Publishers, Inc., Wheaton, IL.

Scripture quotations marked NLT are taken from the Holy Bible, New Living Translation, copyright © 1996, 2004, 2007 by Tyndale House Foundation. Used by permission of Tyndale House Publishers, Inc., Carol Stream, Illinois 60188. All rights reserved.

Scripture quotations marked CEV are taken from the Contemporary English Version. Copyright © 1991, 1992, 1995 by American Bible Society, Used by Permission.

Scripture quotations marked NIV are taken from the Holy Bible, New International Version®, NIV®. Copyright 1973, 1978, 1984, 2011 by Biblica, Inc®. Used by permission of Zondervan. All rights reserved worldwide. www.zondervan.com. The "NIV" and "New International Version" are trademarks registered in the United States Patent and Trademark Office by Biblica, Inc®.

Scripture quotations marked GNT are from the Good News Translation® in Today's English Version – Second Edition Copyright © 1992 by American Bible Society. Used by Permission.

Scripture quotations marked NASB are from the NEW AMERICAN STANDARD BIBLE®, © Copyright 1960, 1962, 1963, 1968, 1971, 1972, 1973, 1975, 1977, 1995 by the Lockman Foundation. Used by permission. (www.lockman.org)

Scripture quotations marked ESV are taken from the ESV Bible® (The Holy Bible, English Standard Version®). Copyright © 2001 by Crossway Bibles, a publishing ministry of Good News Publishers. Used by permission. All rights reserved.

Scripture quotations marked NLV are taken from the *New Life Version*, copyright © 1969 and 2003. Used by permission of Barbour Publishing, Inc., Uhrichsville, Ohio 44683. All rights reserved.Scripture quotations marked NCV are taken from the New Century Version®. Copyright © 2005 by Thomas Nelson, Inc. Used by permission. All rights reserved.

Scripture quotations marked THE MESSAGE are taken from The Message. Copyright © 1993, 1994, 1995, 1996, 2000, 2001, 2002. Used by permission of NavPress Publishing Group.

Scripture quotations marked LEB are taken from the Lexham English Bible. Copyright 2012 Logos Bible Software. Lexham is a registered trademark of Logos Bible Software.

Scripture quotations marked ICB are taken from the International Children's Bible®. Copyright © 1986, 1988, 1999 by Thomas Nelson. Used by permission. All rights reserved.

Scripture quotations marked NRSV are taken from the New Revised Standard Version of the Bible, © 1989. Division of Christian Education, National Council of Churches. Used by permission of Zondervan Publishing House, Licensee.

Written by: Lisa Stilwell

Design by: Suzanne Randolph

Printed in China

Prime: J2101

ISBN: 978-1-64454-660-4

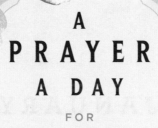

A PRAYER A DAY

FOR MOTHERS

DaySpring

LIVE YOUR FAITH

JANUARY

RENEWAL

REVIVAL OF
THE HEART

The High and Exalted One, who lives
forever, whose name is holy, says this:
"I live in a high and holy place, and with the
oppressed and lowly of spirit, to revive the
spirit of the lowly and revive the
heart of the oppressed."

ISAIAH 57:15

Father, Your presence is all around—
from the heights of the heavens to the
bottoms of the seas. You rejoice in my
victories, and You comfort me in my trials.
Revive me in the year ahead, Lord. Renew
my strength for the coming events. Heal my
wounds from last year's battles, and instill in
me a fresh and new passion for another year
of motherhood in the fullness of Your joy.
In Jesus' name.

AMEN.

TRUST IN HIM

Those who trust in the LORD will renew their
strength; they will soar on wings like eagles;
they will run and not become weary,
they will walk and not faint.

ISAIAH 40:31

Father, I confess I often trust in myself
more than I trust in You, and I get tired!
Please forgive me for putting You second.
I look to You this day and year ahead
with full faith and belief that You are with
me and You will help me with all that I
face much better than I can do on my
own. Knowing this gives me great peace,
assurance, and rest for my spirit, and I
am grateful to know I am not alone.
In Jesus' name.

AMEN.

NEW LIFE

If anyone is in Christ,
he is a new creation;
the old has passed away,
and see, the new has come!

II CORINTHIANS 5:17

Jesus, I am so thankful to know that,
since accepting You as my Savior,
I am no longer the lost and hopeless person
I used to be. You have given me a new start,
a clean slate, and a fresh beginning at life.
In turn, I have given birth and new life and a
fresh beginning in this world to my children.
Help me to balance my roles between
being a parent and being Your child.
I am blessed and honored to be both.
To You be all glory.

AMEN.

A RENEWED SPIRIT

God, create a clean heart for me and
renew a steadfast spirit within me.
PSALM 51:10

Lord, I am so sorry for the ways I fall
short of saying and doing the right things,
especially in front of my family. It's hard not
to let negative thoughts and habits slide
into each day. Please give me a new and
fresh determination to think positively and
to act with pure motives that are consistent
with a testimony that honors You.
In Jesus' name.

AMEN.

PERFECT INSTRUCTION

The instruction of the LORD is perfect,
renewing one's life; the testimony of
the LORD is trustworthy, making the
inexperienced wise.

PSALM 19:7

O Lord, how I love Your Word and the
wisdom I gain each time I read it.
There are answers to my questions and
countless verses expressing Your faithful
love for me. But even more, when I read
through the pages, I hear from Your heart
and get to know You better each day.
Thank You for helping me navigate the
twists and turns of this life of mine.
I would be lost without Your
instruction and help.
In Your name.

AMEN.

INNER RENEWAL

Though our outer self is wasting away,
our inner self is being renewed day by day.
II CORINTHIANS 4:16 ESV

Lord, physical changes from childbirth
and the passing years reveal I'm slowly
changing and getting older, but in the light
of Your love I couldn't feel more alive and
ready to face each new day. Knowing and
serving You brings joy and strength with
a steadfast endurance deep within.
It's an energy and passion that nothing
else compares to. You are an awesome God.
In Your precious name.
AMEN.

FULFILLING
HIS PURPOSE

Turn my eyes away from vanity
[all those worldly, meaningless things
that distract—let Your priorities be mine],
and restore me [with renewed
energy] in Your ways.

PSALM 119:37 AMP

Yes, Lord, please do turn my eyes away
from all that doesn't matter in light of
eternity. Trying to be the perfect mom
saps my energy, but fulfilling my purpose
in You gives renewed passion and strength.
Guide me in the way of Your truth and keep
me in the center of what matters most
to You and to my family.

AMEN.

NEW BIRTH

He saved us because of His mercy,
and not because of any good things
that we have done. God washed us by
the power of the Holy Spirit.
He gave us new birth and a fresh beginning.
TITUS 3:5 CEV

Father, I know that only because of Your
mercy and grace can I live free and
empowered by Your Spirit within me.
The past no longer has power to influence
or control my thoughts and actions.
Help me to let go of yesterday and walk
with You today as my only Source for
experiencing the best life possible.
For this I lift all praise to You.
AMEN.

NEW
MIRACLES

The crowd marveled as they saw the mute
speaking, the crippled restored, and the
lame walking, and the blind seeing; and
they glorified the God of Israel.

MATTHEW 15:31 NASB

Lord, You are a God of miracles.
Whether the brokenness is physical,
emotional, relational, or spiritual, You make
us whole.. I ask today for Your compassion
to reach down and work in my life—to heal
the bruises I carry in my heart and to help
heal bruises I may have caused my child.
Fill me with Your peace and understanding.
Revive Your Spirit within me so it burns
with a flame that cannot be quenched
no matter what I face.
In Jesus' name.
AMEN.

LIVE IN TODAY

Because of the Lᴏʀᴅ's faithful love
we do not perish, for His mercies never end.
They are new every morning;
great is Your faithfulness!
LAMENTATIONS 3:22-23

Lord, thank You that every morning is a
fresh new start—for walking in obedience
to You, for blessing my family and others,
for praying for my children and those who
need a prayer, and for embracing Your holy
presence in my life. Yesterday is over and
behind. Help me to move forward and live
this day in the fullness of Your grace.

AMEN.

TRANSFORMED FROM WITHIN

Put to death what belongs to your earthly nature...You are being renewed in knowledge according to the image of your Creator.

COLOSSIANS 3:5,10

Father, I want to stop responding to old, unhealthy habits and start living in a way that shows new self-discipline. You are the whole of my life and the reason I am truly alive. Make Your ways the desires of my heart, and give me strength to overcome the strongholds that have kept me from experiencing true freedom in You.
In Christ's name I pray.

AMEN.

CLEANSED FROM SIN

Be gracious to me, God, according to
Your faithful love; according to
Your abundant compassion,
blot out my rebellion.
Completely wash away my guilt
and cleanse me from my sin.

PSALM 51:1-2

Father, I confess to You and ask Your
forgiveness for the ways I try to live
for myself instead of for You. Why do I
continually get off track and do things my
way instead of looking to You first?
Please forgive me and cleanse my heart.
I want to be ever so sensitive to the leading
of Your Spirit and carry a willingness to do,
say, and go Your way—on Your terms.
In Jesus' name I pray.

AMEN.

HE REVIVES
THE SPIRIT

God, who is like You? You caused me to
experience many troubles and misfortunes,
but You will revive me again.
You will bring me up again,
even from the depths of the earth.
PSALM 71:19-20 HCSB

Lord, I don't always understand why You
allow hardship in my life, but I trust You.
I believe You to be a good Father, and I
know that You are with me to lead and
guide, heal and restore. I walk in faith that
You will redeem what I think is lost, and
that You will revive my spirit with renewed
strength, purpose, and meaning—
all for Your glory.
In Jesus' name.
AMEN.

A NEW MIND

Do not be conformed to this age,
but be transformed by the renewing of
your mind, so that you may discern what is
the good, pleasing, and perfect will of God.

ROMANS 12:2

Father, I confess I get distracted by the voices of this world that pull me away from You and Your will. It's a battle not to be fought on my own logic and ideas. Please, drown out anything that is not of You. I want to hear Your voice and know just what You want for me and my family today and the next. Give me wisdom and guide my steps so I'm able to point my children to You in a way that excites them and draws their hearts to You.
In Jesus' name.

AMEN.

TODAY IS
A NEW DAY

Have nothing to do with your old sinful life.
It was sinful because of being fooled
into following bad desires.
Let your minds and hearts be made new.

EPHESIANS 4:22–23 NLV

Lord, help me to turn away from the bad
memories that creep into my mind and
dispel the thoughts that bring heaviness
and shame. Today is a new day, and
knowing You means knowing freedom from
past mistakes. I claim my freedom now and
pray that You will guard my heart and mind
from the enemy's attempts to rob me of
the peace that is mine in You. I walk afresh
today with You in my sights. Thank You,
Jesus, for giving me true freedom.
In Your name I pray.

AMEN.

A CLEAN HEART

As a face is reflected in water,
so the heart reflects the real person.
PROVERBS 27:19 NLT

Father, I want my life to reflect a pure
and clean heart that loves You. Show me
any ways I am not being true to You, to
myself, or to my family. Help me to examine
my motives for the things I do and the
conversations I have. Give me a humble
heart that is fueled by a desire to serve
and pray for others. Guard my heart from
the enemy's tactics. Mend my heart so it's
whole and strong and filled with Your joy.
Help me to radiate Your love to my family
so that they see You and feel at peace.
In Your name I pray.
AMEN.

NEW HEIGHTS OF TRUST

Early in the morning before the sun is up,
I am praying and pointing out
how much I trust in You.

PSALM 119:147 TLB

O Lord, how I love You. I come to You this day releasing my anxious thoughts and entrusting my needs to Your care. You have provided so abundantly in the past; please increase my faith to trust You more than ever with my cares for the future. Fill me with Your peace that passes understanding, and help me walk through this day in full confidence that I can trust You completely in every detail.

To You, Jesus, I pray.

AMEN.

A NEW WORK

*It is God who works in you to will and
to act in order to fulfill His good purpose.*
PHILIPPIANS 2:13 NIV

Lord, help me to apply Your Word to my
everyday, routine life. Help me make this
a discipline of the mind and heart so I am
transformed little by little into Your likeness.
Keep me going, give me strength, and help
me to fulfill my calling as a mother.
I don't even want to try living without
knowing You are here with me to help
in exactly the ways I need.
In Jesus' name I pray.
AMEN.

A NEW START

You were washed, you were sanctified,
you were justified in the name of the Lord
Jesus Christ and by the Spirit of our God.

I CORINTHIANS 6:11 NIV

Father, I am so grateful to You for
sending Your Son and displaying the most
beautiful act of love known to the world.
Because of Jesus' sacrifice, I am whole.
My transgressions no longer have a hold
on me. I am free of sin's stain and sealed
by Your Spirit. Amidst all the chaos and
busyness in my life, I pause to worship and
praise Your name for such a gift.
Thank You for the assurance of Your
faithful love and healing grace.

AMEN.

WASHED CLEAN

Let us come near to God with a sincere heart and a sure faith, with hearts that have been purified from a guilty conscience and with bodies washed with clean water.

HEBREWS 10:22 GNT

Lord, I come to You today with a humble and sincere heart, praising Your goodness and willingness to clean up all that I'm guilty of. The power of Your Spirit to clear my conscience makes me a walking miracle each and every day. I look to You now and walk in faith that You are with me, filling me with Your love and grace and newness of heart. I want to be a mom that is filled with Your joy and love, who pours out the same into each little heart.

In Jesus' name.

AMEN.

A CLEAN HEART

God, who knows the heart,
bore witness to them with [the Gentiles]
by giving them the Holy Spirit...
cleansing their hearts by faith.

ACTS 15:8-9

Lord, thank You for the gift of Your
Holy Spirit. I want this year to be a time of
going where Your Spirit leads and living in
the abundance of Your grace. Cleanse my
heart of all that would hinder Your voice or
cause me to stumble. I want only to see
and hear You above all else.
All praise be to You.

AMEN.

HE KNOWS
THE FUTURE

The LORD will always lead you,
satisfy you in a parched land,
and strengthen your bones.
You will be like a watered garden and
like a spring whose water never runs dry.
ISAIAH 58:11

Father, sometimes being a mom is hard. Thinking on this new year ahead, I can't see how plans will turn out, but You can, and I trust that You will provide as each need arises. Please go before me. Lead me so that no matter how difficult circumstances may get, I have steadfast hope and assurance that my family and I will remain in Your care. I love You and thank You for Your goodness.

AMEN.

HIS WELLSPRING OF LIFE

[The people] are filled from the abundance
of Your house. You let them drink
from Your refreshing stream.
For the wellspring of life is with You.

PSALM 36:8-9

Lord, You are my wellspring of life to draw
from each day. And as I do, I am renewed—
with new hope, new strength, and new eyes
to see just how almighty You are. Thank You
for filling me with the blessing of Your joy
and the warmth of Your love. Help me to be
the same for my children.
In Jesus' name.

AMEN.

A NEW SONG

I waited patiently for the LORD, and He
turned to me and heard my cry for help.
He brought me up from a desolate pit...
making my steps secure. He put a new song
in my mouth, a hymn of praise to our God.

PSALM 40:1-3

Father, I am so filled with praise for You
today. When I look back from where
You've brought me, I am amazed at the
transformation of my life. You raised me
up from despair and placed me in the
embrace of Your loving arms. In You I have
hope and peace that well up so much,
I cannot stop praising You. Thank You for
putting a new song in my heart.

AMEN.

A NEW
WORK

Lᴏʀᴅ, You are our Father;
we are the clay, and You are our potter;
we all are the work of Your hands.

ISAIAH 64:8

Lord, my life and my children's lives,
are all Yours. Help me fill my mom shoes
with the confidence that You are constantly
at work and in control. I know sometimes
I fall short and get tired, but I want my life
to reveal the touch of Your hands and the
power of what You can and will do in spite
of the challenges. Make me a vessel that
can withstand the heat and pressures that
are sure to come, as well as a source
where Your love can flow freely
onto those around me.
To You be all glory.
AMEN.

NO MORE STAIN

All the prophets testify about Him,
that through His name everyone who
believes in Him [whoever trusts in and
relies on Him, accepting Him as Savior and
Messiah] receives forgiveness of sins.

ACTS 10:43 AMP

Heavenly Father, I trust in You.
I believe that Jesus died for my sins and
covers me now with His grace. It's a gift
to know that when I confess my sin, Your
mercy reaches down and removes the stain
and guilt that could otherwise be. You give
me hope for a future in eternity with You,
and for this my heart is full and rejoices
at the sound of Your name.

AMEN.

RENEWED HOPE

When doubts filled my mind,
Your comfort gave me
renewed hope and cheer.

PSALM 94:19 NLT

Lord, Your faithful love is a lifeline for me.
Sometimes doubt pours into my mind
because I can't see how circumstances
will turn out, and I don't know what to do
except call on You. So I'm calling out to
You now. Please hear my cry and surround
me with Your peace. Forgive me for ever
doubting Your ability to work out all things
for my good and Your glory. I want to soak
in the comfort You so willingly provide and
rest in renewed hope as I trust in You.
All praise to You.

AMEN.

GENUINE FULLFILLMENT

Sons [and daughters] are indeed a heritage from the LORD, offspring, a reward.
PSALM 127:3

Lord, you are a God of miracles, including the miracle of a child's birth. I am so grateful for each new baby You bring into this world, and I'm especially grateful for mine. Thank You for the privilege of raising a new little being to know You and to be a shining light of sweetness in this world. My badge of honor is MOM, and I couldn't be happier.

AMEN.

NEW PATHS

A person's heart plans his way,
but the LORD determines his steps.

PROVERBS 16:9

Yes, Lord, I have plans for the year ahead,
but I want You to be the Master of them all.
Show me which ones to pursue and which
to disregard, which to nurture and which to
put away for another time. I want Your way
to shine brighter than the steps I've set for
myself, so I put both palms up and release
to You my will in exchange for Yours.
Have Your way with me, Lord.
In Jesus' name.

AMEN.

REDEEMING GRACE

*Our Father in heaven, Your name
be honored as holy. Your kingdom come.
Your will be done on earth as it is in heaven.*

MATTHEW 6:9-10

Father, I honor Your name and look to
Your will for my life. Help me to live one
day at a time in light of Your overall
plans, not just for me but for my family
too. I pray in reverence and awe as I look
to Your Son, Jesus, and the redeeming
grace He provides. I confess I am nothing
without You, and that with You I can live in
complete victory. Hallelujah! I lift my praise
and worship to Your holy name.

AMEN.

HE REBUILDS

The God of all grace, who called you to His eternal glory in Christ, will Himself restore, establish, strengthen, and support you after you have suffered a little while.

I PETER 5:10

Lord, I am so grateful to know that no matter what's been lost due to my mistakes, my failed health, or someone else's actions, You are a redeeming God. You promise to rebuild and empower, refresh and make new for Your continued purpose.
Help me to entrust my circumstances to You now and to live forward in new grace and new mercy as You establish my feet on unshakable ground.
In Jesus I pray.

AMEN.

FEBRUARY

LOVE

THE FULLNESS
OF HIS LOVE

I want you to know all about Christ's love,
although it is too wonderful to be
measured. Then your lives will be
filled with all that God is.

EPHESIANS 3:19 CEV

Father, You are greater than life.
No other source of love has filled my
heart, soul, and mind the way You have.
I know Your love is sincere and eternal as it
points to Jesus' death on the cross not only
for me but also for my children. Help me to
teach them about Your sacrifice, as well as
be a vessel of Your love so that You
become real to them.
In Your sweet name.

AMEN.

COMPLETE LOVE

Love the LORD your God
with all your heart, with all your soul,
and with all your strength.
DEUTERONOMY 6:5 GNT

Lord, I put You on the throne of my heart
today. I know this means putting my wants
and plans down and living completely for
You. Help me to know just how to do that
with so many demands pulling at me.
I know I struggle with doing things my way
rather than Your, so I ask for Your help. You
are a Father to the fatherless, a Husband
to the widow, a Friend to those who know
You—including me, and I am
so grateful. All praise be to You.
AMEN.

GLIMPSES OF HIS LOVE

Your steadfast love is before my eyes,
and I walk in faithfulness to You.

PSALM 26:3 NRSV

Father, I look around and see touches
of Your love everywhere. In my child's
eyes, in the extra strength You give when
I need it, in Your mercy when I blow
it—Your presence is abundant. I walk in
faithfulness to You today the best I know
how. I pray and sing to You with praise and
thanksgiving, and I open my heart to let in
Your love and, in turn, love on my family.
In Christ's name.

AMEN.

JEALOUS LOVE

The LORD your God, who is among you, is a jealous God.

DEUTERONOMY 6:15

Lord, it is sometimes hard to fathom
that You are present with me at this very
moment. You, God, are with me when I rise,
when I work, when I sleep, when I try to
sleep but can't. You hear my thoughts and
eagerly receive my cries for help.
Thank You for such a height of love that
You are jealous when too much of my
attention goes to others and to things
and activities that don't fulfill or complete
me as You do. In Your warm embrace
is where I want to be.

AMEN.

SPEAKING LOVE

Praising and cursing come out of the same mouth.... Can a fig tree produce olives... or a grapevine produce figs? Neither can a saltwater spring yield fresh water.

JAMES 3:10, 12 HCSB

O Lord, I know that losing my temper and being critical are contrary to the love You tell me to extend to others, especially to my family. Please put a guard and filter over my mouth, and help me to speak only what is edifying, uplifting, and encouraging to my children. Give me patience and help me to see the good in them the way You do. Help me to highlight that which will bless each heart in just the way they need.

AMEN.

MOTIVATED BY LOVE

Let everything you do be done in love
[motivated and inspired by
God's love for us].

I CORINTHIANS 16:14 AMP

Father, as I go through this day, help me to
have pure motives in my actions and words.
Help me to put "self" aside and really see
the root needs around me. Give me a heart
of compassion for reaching out and truly
loving others—my family, my neighbors—
through service or encouragement, even if
all I do is make eye contact and smile.
Help me to make a difference in how they
see You—a God who is so very good.
Praise to Your holy name.

AMEN.

HIS LOVE IS THERE

Blessed be the LORD, for He has wondrously
shown His faithful love to me
in a city under siege.
PSALM 31:21

Lord, this world can be frightening.
Headlines read of attacks and killings,
and chaos is rampant. It seems that
wherever I look, there is a family under
siege—sometimes even my own. Help me
to remember that Your love abounds.
It shines brighter than my best of days and
is a beacon of hope on the scary ones.
Your love is greater than all the turmoil I
see. It's there for whenever and however I
need. Thank You from my heart!
AMEN.

LOVE YOUR ENEMIES

I say to you, Love your enemies and
pray for those who persecute you.
MATTHEW 5:44 ESV

O Lord, this is Your command,
but I confess it's hard. Help me, please,
to actually do it. The next time I'm
tempted to retaliate toward someone who's
offended me, remind me to take a breath
and choose love. You aren't telling me to
do anything You don't do Yourself.
Help me to remember that there's always
a bigger plan with a deeper meaning than
what I see in any given moment.
And help me to really grasp the depth of
love You have for me, especially on days
when I know I disappoint You.
In Jesus' name.
AMEN.

START WITH LOVE

*The Spirit produces love, joy, peace,
patience, kindness, goodness,
faithfulness, humility, and self-control.*
GALATIANS 5:22–23 GNT

Lord, it is obvious I cannot love out of my
own willpower—it comes from You and
the power of Your Spirit within me. So if I
want more love, I simply need more of You.
Please hear me now and fill my thoughts
with Your truth. Help me to share Your love
from the overflow of Your presence in my
heart. I want to exude all the fruit of the
Spirit, but love is where it begins, so I begin
this day professing my love of You.
In Your wonderful name.
AMEN.

THE FATHER'S LOVE

See what great love the Father has
given us that we should be called
God's children—and we are!

I JOHN 3:1

Father, it's no less than amazing to think
that I am Your child—baggage, problems,
hang-ups, bad habits, and all.
You took me in and now call me Your own.
I'm adopted into Your family and sealed
with the promise of hope and a future.
I rejoice today for Your presence in my life,
in my home, in my children's hearts.
As I live and grow in Your family,
You live and grow in mine.
Thank You for such a gift!

AMEN.

WITHOUT LOVE

If I speak human or angelic tongues
but do not have love, I am a noisy gong
or a clanging cymbal.

I CORINTHIANS 13:1

Lord, I know that I can care for my children,
do all the mom stuff, and say prayers on
behalf of each family member, but if I do it
going through the motions and not with a
sincere heart, the effects fall short of what
could be. The point of tending to each
scraped knee, responding to endless requests,
and trying to provide some structure for
each day isn't so I'll look like a mom who has
everything together, it's to bring You alive and
to spread Your love to those I love the most.
Convict my heart when love is not at the core
and in the lead. I want to keep You at the
forefront of what I say and do.

AMEN.

OBEDIENT LOVE

Love means doing what God has commanded us, and He has commanded us to love one another.

II JOHN 1:6 NLT

Father, if I say I love You, that means I
should willingly do what You say,
even when I don't feel like it. I think of how
I feel when my child doesn't obey me;
I can only imagine how You—God—feel
when I disregard Your Word. So much of
the time I get busy and am spread so thin
that I don't have the time to stop and really
love others, my family, my children the way
You want me to. Please forgive me and
help me to remember that Your blessings
are far greater than any checked-off to-do
list will ever be.
In Your name I pray.

AMEN.

SUSTAINING LOVE

As God's ministers, we commend ourselves
in everything: by great endurance,
by afflictions...by patience,
by kindness... by sincere love.

II CORINTHIANS 6:4, 6

Father, this verse reminds me of the song "They Will Know We Are Christians by Our Love." Allowing Your Spirit to do the unexplainable by sustaining me through trials, by enabling me to sincerely love when one of my children is defiant or challenging—it all brings attention to You and the Christian faith. Help me to remember this. Fill me with Your love overflowing so that I can pour it out to the point of standing out for Your glory.

AMEN.

SACRIFICIAL LOVE

For God loved the world in this way:
He gave His one and only Son,
so that everyone who believes in Him
will not perish but have eternal life.

JOHN 3:16

Your love, O Lord, surpasses all other loves
in life. To sacrifice Your Son as an offering
for my sins is the greatest love gift of
all. Words cannot describe my heartfelt
thanks—for giving me new life, a new
purpose, and a new day today in which to
live. I am so grateful and humbled,
blessed and filled, with nothing but
praise for You this day.
I exalt Your name.

AMEN.

UNSHAKABLE LOVE

"Though the mountains move and the hills shake, My love will not be removed from you and My covenant of peace will not be shaken," says your compassionate LORD.

ISAIAH 54:10

Father, there are times when life moves and shakes the ground from underneath my feet, and all I can do is hang on. It is so very comforting to know that no matter how big the quakes or how strong the tremors, Your love remains the same—secure within my heart. This sustains my will to keep going with courage and confidence that all will be well.
All thanks and praise to You.

AMEN.

HIGH ROAD
TO LOVE

Hatred stirs up conflicts,
but love covers all offenses.
PROVERBS 10:12

Father, with all the conflict in news
headlines, this truth rings louder and
clearer than ever. Help me take Your high
road to love, even when I'm offended or
disagree. Help me to love instead of lash,
to be silent instead of spew. I want to be
peace on Your behalf and have a heart of
love so that the evidence of Your grace will
be seen by all who are around me today.
I ask this in the name and power of Jesus.

AMEN.

CHOSEN LOVE

God loves you and has chosen you as His own special people. So be gentle, kind, humble, meek, and patient.

COLOSSIANS 3:12 CEV

Lord, to know that I am special to You takes my breath away. When I stop to receive the warmth of Your presence, I am filled with peace that passes understanding. Thank You for this. Keep my heart humble. Instill in me the kindness and compassion You would show the hurting. Help me stay in Your sweet spot of love so the fruit of gentleness and patience will be an outpouring of blessing to my family. All glory to You, Jesus.

AMEN.

FAITHFUL LOVE

May Your faithful love rest on us, LORD,
for we put our hope in You.

PSALM 33:22

Father, the thought of Your love resting
on me brings such calm to my soul.
And it's much needed not only because of
the unrest that comes from the world and
life in general, but from the overwhelming
demands I face each day. There is no other
option in my heart and mind than to keep
looking to You and drawing from the love
that You give in such abundance. You are
ever present and ready to help, and I love
You for Your faithfulness to me.
You are worthy of all praise.

AMEN.

HIS
LOVING-KINDNESS

As for me, I shall sing of Your strength;
yes, I shall joyfully sing of Your
lovingkindness in the morning, for You
have been my stronghold and a refuge
in the day of my distress.

PSALM 59:16 NASB

Lord, I look to You, and my heart is filled
with gladness and relief. You have been
good and faithful to provide, protect,
comfort, and bring favor to all corners of
my life in the past, and You will do the same
today and in my future. You put a new
strength in my heart and remain a refuge to
which I can run. I am filled with praise and
thanksgiving—nothing else compares to You.
In Your holy name I pray.

AMEN.

GENTLE LOVE

The kingdom of God is not a matter of
talk but of power. What do you want?
Should I come to you with a rod,
or in love and a spirit of gentleness?

I CORINTHIANS 4:20-21

Lord, this is easy to answer: I want Your
love and a spirit of gentleness! You are love,
and love is power—the greatest force in all
of humanity. When I wrong someone,
I want to be corrected with gentleness,
so help me extend the same response to
my family when I become frustrated or
offended. Help me to stop threatening and
start doing, to stop thinking in my head
and start acting from my heart.
Let love rule in me this day.
In Jesus' name.

AMEN.

EXPRESSIONS
OF LOVE

My lips will glorify You because
Your faithful love is better than life.

PSALM 63:3

Father, Your love is faithful—it's always
been there to hold me together, no matter
the time of day or night. Many times I don't
even deserve it, yet it is there. You love me
even when I don't always love You back,
which is humbling. So I will praise You with
lifted arms today; I will sing and worship to
express the best I can the immense
joy You bring to my heart.
You deserve all glory.
You alone are worthy.

AMEN.

HIS LOVE
IS PATIENT

Love is patient.
I CORINTHIANS 13:4

Lord, I'm so grateful for Your patience when I am slow to respond to Your leading or when I get short-tempered with my family. So often I hear You telling me to do things, yet I get around to them when I feel like it rather than when You say. At the same time, I'm guilty of being impatient with my family when they don't move fast enough or do things the way I want them done. Please help me to be patient and kind today to the same degree that I need patience and kindness myself. Keep my heart humble and help me to remember that love has the power to heal the most stressful and broken situations. In Your name.

AMEN.

WHAT LOVE IS NOT

*Love...is not boastful,
is not arrogant, is not rude.*
I CORINTHIANS 13:4-5

O Lord, when I am honest with myself,
there are times I boast about my
accomplishments as a mother.
It's hard doing so much for my family
with sometimes very little recognition and
appreciation. Help me to remember that,
ultimately, it is You I am serving and living
for. Please remove any pride and replace
it with pure and simple humility and a
quickness to give You the glory where
glory is due. I know that all I accomplish is
because of Your love and grace over my life.
With gratefulness I pray.
AMEN.

LOVE PUTS JESUS FIRST

[Love] is not self-seeking.
I CORINTHIANS 13:5

Father, there is a constant battle within to do my will rather than Yours. I want to go my way, fulfill my dreams, and do it all on my timeline. But it's a battle because I sincerely want to do Your will and fulfill Your calling and purpose. Please help me put self aside and remain focused with a full heart of assurance that You know what is best for me and my family. Help me to truly trust that Your ways hold blessings beyond what I could ever accomplish for myself.
In Jesus' name.
AMEN.

LOVE IS A CLEAN SLATE

[Love] does not keep a record of wrongs.

I CORINTHIANS 13:5

Father, I am so thankful and relieved that
ungodly things I did years ago, or even
as recently as yesterday, are forgiven.
You don't hold them over my head.
They are wiped away and forgotten.
This is a concept that's hard to fully grasp,
because I do the opposite—I often keep
records of what I've done or how people
have hurt or offended me. Help me to
forgive and look forward, not backward.
Help me to extend the same grace to
them that You extend to me.
In the power of Jesus, I pray.

AMEN.

LOVE IS TRUTH

Love...rejoices in the truth.
I CORINTHIANS 13:6

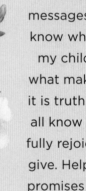

Lord, there are so many conflicting messages in this world. Sometimes I don't know what to think, let alone how to help my children know what to think. This is what makes me love and trust Your Word: it is truth. You are Truth. And the more we all know You, the more we can thrive and fully rejoice in the power and freedom You give. Help me today to learn more of Your promises and remember to claim them for myself and my children.

All praise be to You.

AMEN.

LOVE BEARS ALL THINGS

[Love] bears all things.
I CORINTHIANS 13:7

Father, sometimes life gets very hard, and I want to give up. I struggle to deal with temper tantrums, endless demands, and often thankless work. Sometimes it seems easier to run. But I know that love stays and bears all things—the way You stay and cover me in all the ways I fall short of Your purposes for me. Thank You for holding on to me and promising never to let go. Help me to do the same, especially with those I love the most.
In Jesus' name.
AMEN.

LOVE NEVER ENDS

Love never ends.
I CORINTHIANS 13:8

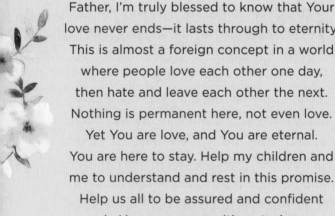

Father, I'm truly blessed to know that Your
love never ends—it lasts through to eternity.
This is almost a foreign concept in a world
where people love each other one day,
then hate and leave each other the next.
Nothing is permanent here, not even love.
Yet You are love, and You are eternal.
You are here to stay. Help my children and
me to understand and rest in this promise.
Help us all to be assured and confident
in Your presence with us today,
tomorrow, and the next.
In Your name I pray.
AMEN.

SINCERE LOVE

Above all, maintain constant love
for one another, since love covers
a multitude of sins.

I PETER 4:8

Lord, help me to live out this day in Your
love. As I work, shop, drive the kids,
and eat, help me to remain in a spirit of love
toward each person I greet. Help me to be
all there with each encounter and to extend
grace the same way You so lavishly extend
it to me. Help me to keep love higher than
any box I want to check on my to-do list.
In Your faithful love I pray.

AMEN.

MARCH

STRENGTH

THE RIGHT FOCUS

He gives strength to the faint and strengthens the powerless.

ISAIAH 40:29

Lord, I am tired! Being a mom and always having to be "on" is so draining and exhausting at times. I escape into Your arms right now and breathe in the strength and rest that I need to face this day. Help me be in a state of calm and not worry about getting everything done. Help me to focus on what's most important and let the rest go. Don't let me miss the joy of my kids and the love they have for life.
In Your name I pray.
AMEN.

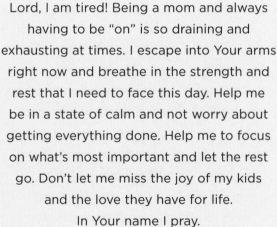

HIS WAYS ARE BEST

You shall keep all the commandments
which I am commanding you today, so
that you may be strong and go in and
take possession of the land which you are
crossing over [the Jordan] to possess.

DEUTERONOMY 11:8 AMP

O Lord, this is very convicting: When I follow
Your ways and do as You lead, I will have
more strength. But the temptation to create
and follow my own agenda is so great.
Help me to trust that You hold my family's
and my best interests close to Your heart,
and that You will not steer us wrong.
Help me to let go of what I want and
embrace Your plans with confidence
and renewed strength.
In Your great name.
AMEN.

DAILY CARE

Now please listen to your servant.
Let me set some food in front of you.
Eat and it will give you strength
so you can go on your way.
I SAMUEL 28:22

Father, this is a good reminder of the importance of self-care. I often forget to care for my own basic needs, yet when I do, I know I'm better and stronger to care for my family. Help me to learn good balance— when to give and when to stop and replenish myself. Help me not feel guilty for feeding my own soul and my own body with moments away from the constant demands. I ask You now to let me be still in Your love and rest as I face this day.
Thank You, Jesus.
AMEN.

HIS STRENGTH, YOUR STRENGTH

David was in an extremely difficult
position.... But [he] found strength
in the LORD his God.
I SAMUEL 30:6

Lord, it is hard not to worry about
the difficulties I face. The dynamics of
motherhood are many—much more than
I ever knew or prepared for. Worry is
draining, and fretting is so nonproductive,
yet I often find myself doing just that. I look
to You today with faith and hope in my
heart that all will be well. I believe You are
with me in every twist and turn, and that
Your strength will enable me to accomplish
more than I ever could on my own.
With thanksgiving and praise.

AMEN.

STRENGTH FOR THE BATTLES

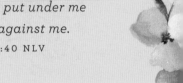

You have dressed me with strength
for battle. You have put under me
those who came against me.
II SAMUEL 22:40 NLV

Lord, as I face this new day, I know there
will be hiccups and challenges, especially
with having a child to raise and teach,
care for and love. Please clothe me with
Your armor. Instill in me the strength You
know I'll need for remaining unmoved no
matter what happens. I'm so grateful You
do not leave me or any of us alone to our
circumstances. I commit to walking in Your
presence with all of my heart.
In Jesus' name.
AMEN.

GOD, YOUR STRONGHOLD

The LORD is the strength of His people;
He is a stronghold of salvation
for His anointed.

PSALM 28:8

Lord, You are my stronghold.
Not my friends, not my home, not my job.
You are my strong tower for facing my
life, and today I feel overwhelmed thinking
about all there is to do. Bring my thoughts
back around to one thing: the gift of my
salvation. Help me refocus, not on my list,
but on Your promises to help and uphold,
to will and to act in ways that are pleasing
to You. This is the day that You have made,
I want to rejoice and be glad in it because
it's the most important thing.

AMEN.

OKAY TO SAY NO

A wise warrior is better than a strong one, and a man of knowledge than one of strength.

PROVERBS 24:5

Lord, this verse reminds me of the concept of working smarter, not harder. This means prioritizing my day and making sure my plans align with Yours. Give me wisdom for what to do today and what to do tomorrow or not even do at all. The simple thinking that it's okay to say no to some things lightens my spirit and energizes my mood. Be my lead and my guide. Help me to know my next steps. In Jesus' sweet name.

AMEN.

WE NEED EACH OTHER

[Paul] set out, traveling through one place after another in the region of Galatia and Phrygia, strengthening all the disciples.

ACTS 18:23

Father, I know I'm not the only mom who struggles with an overwhelming list of activities and needs to fill. There are a lot of others who battle with the same balancing act. Help me to be an encouragement and to be creative in how we might help each other—cover each other—so that we can benefit from our strength in numbers. None of us are meant to do life alone, and certainly not I. We all need You and each other. Thank You for this reminder.

AMEN.

HOLY ENERGY

*Don't stay far away, L*ORD*!*
My strength comes from You,
so hurry and help.
PSALM 22:19 CEV

Lord, I know when I'm guilty of trying to do things in my own strength, because that's when I get burned out. My attitude suffers and I seem to get less done rather than more. I am crying out to You now asking for Your help. I need You—to lift me up and instill in me a fresh wave of energy to get me through this day. Help me to eliminate what isn't necessary and to focus on what matters most. Thank You for Your patience while I try to find the right balance that works for who You created me to be. In Your great name.

AMEN.

HIS JOY IS A REFUGE

*I will sing of Your strength and will joyfully
proclaim Your faithful love in the morning.
For You have been a stronghold for me, a
refuge in my day of trouble.*

PSALM 59:16

Lord, I praise You today and lift up a song
from my soul for Your goodness to my my
dear family and to me. Your love blesses
me like no other, and I am filled with joy—
Your joy—because of Your faithfulness.
You are a refuge and a safe and pleasant
place to rest my weary heart day after day.
When I am in Your arms, I feel such relief
from the pressures of this world and the
weight of all there is to do. I love You and
praise Your holy name with thanksgiving.

AMEN.

GAZE ON HIM

God, You are my God; I eagerly seek You....
I gaze on You in the sanctuary
to see Your strength and Your glory.

PSALM 63:1-2

Father, I love that whenever I look to You,
my anxieties decrease. Your presence,
Your power are so remarkably greater
than any mountains I face right now. I love
that I serve a great and mighty God who
is with me, to carry and to help even in
the smallest of details. Your glory is my
strength and my shield that I cling to with
full confidence and assurance that today
is going to be a great day.
Praise Your holy name.

AMEN.

STRENGTH IN TRUST

Don't be conceited, sure of your own wisdom.
Instead, trust and reverence the LORD...
when you do that, then you will be given
renewed health and vitality.

PROVERBS 3:7-8 TLB

Ah, Lord, sometimes I don't understand
why I feel tired—I seem to be doing all the
right things to ensure good health.
Yet I do often think and plan for what I
want and what I think should be, and that
alone creates such a heavy burden to
manage. So I open my hands and release
my plans and trust in what You want for this
day—both for me and the little souls You've
given to be in my care. I love You and thank
You for the promise of Your strength.

AMEN.

PROTECTING THE INNOCENT

"Not by strength or by might, but by My Spirit," says the LORD *of Armies.*

ZECHARIAH 4:6

Father, it is a constant battle to protect my child from the dark forces of this world. To guard innocent eyes and ears from words and images promoting love of things and phony and insincere people is a full-time job. I pray for Your supernatural intervention to help me protect and quickly discern when something harmful is trying to make its way into my home. I pray for Your Spirit to be in this place—to cover my family with love and comfort, purity and peace.

Thank You, Lord.

AMEN.

QUIET STRENGTH

Strength and honor are her clothing,
and she can laugh at the time to come.
PROVERBS 31:25

Lord, I love that quiet strength and honor
are mine because of Your presence in my
heart. And I love how my trust in You truly
does instill confidence about the future.
I have nothing to fret or worry about
because You are in control. These are gifts
far greater than any "thing" can give.
And You give these blessings because You
know they are needed for raising children
to know and love You above anything else
this world has to offer. You are so good
to me, and I thank You for being a very
present help at all times.
In Jesus' name.
AMEN.

SERVING HIM DAILY

*If anyone serves, let it be from the strength
God provides, so that God may be glorified
through Jesus Christ in everything.*

I PETER 4:11

Father, sometimes I forget that, with
tending to all the needs of my family—
folding piles of laundry, cooking meals
and packing lunches, giving hugs and
kissing bruises, listening to school-day
drama stories—I am ultimately serving You.
Sometimes it feels like a thankless job,
but I am reminded here that I couldn't do
it without You. And You are the One who
really gets the glory. I wouldn't want it any
other way. All glory and praise to You.

AMEN.

LET HIS
LIGHT SHINE

*The Lord stood with me and
strengthened me, so that I might
fully preach the word and all
the Gentiles might hear it.*

II TIMOTHY 4:17

Lord, please stand with me now
and throughout this day as I teach
and talk about You to my children.
Let my energy and love for You shine
without fail to young and innocent minds
that are hungry to learn and eager to love
and be loved. Help every ounce of godly
influence that dwells in me to flow out of
my mouth and my actions and be a
light that shines toward You.
All praise to You.

AMEN.

SPEAK UP

*Always be prepared to give an answer
to everyone who asks you to give the
reason for the hope that you have.*

I PETER 3:15 NIV

Lord, so often when I have conversations
with a nonbeliever, I dodge the topic of faith.
I don't like conflict or rejection, yet my heart
gets heavy for not speaking up at opportune
times. Please help me overcome this fear.
You are the One I want to please, and I
need Your strength and courage not to be
ashamed of the gospel—ever. It's how I want
my children to be as well. I want to put my
love for You over my fear of rejection from
people. Help me be prepared and bold when
I know You want me to speak up.
To You I lift my eyes.

AMEN.

STAND FIRM

I will not be afraid of ten thousands of
people who stand all around against me.

PSALM 3:6 NLV

Lord, when faced with choices of education, after-school activities, digital devices, and forms of discipline, I often feel I'm going against the current of this world. Even in Christian circles there can be pressure to conform to certain beliefs that don't sit right with me. I know my child better than anyone on this earth except You. Give me the strength I need to stand firm in my beliefs in spite of what others think I should do. I only want to please You and bless my family with what's best for us all.
In Jesus' name.

AMEN.

NO MORE JUDGING

Do not judge, so that you won't be judged.
MATTHEW 7:1

Lord, I don't like to be judged by the way
I parent my children, yet I confess there
are times I judge other moms for their
choice of methods. Help me remember
that, just because a child acts out, it
doesn't mean I or other moms are doing
anything wrong. We, for the most part,
are doing the best we can. Give me the
strength and determination to offer support
and encouragement instead of a raised
judgmental brow. Parenting is not easy.
Help me to think only of edifying my sisters
so we all can feel Your love and support.
In Jesus' name.
AMEN.

LOVE CORRECTS

A refusal to correct is a refusal to love;
love your children by disciplining them.
PROVERBS 13:24 THE MESSAGE

Lord, when one of my children is defiant
or disrespectful, I know there should be a
consequence to correct the behavior.
But it's hard to always know how or what to
do. I often want to give in when I see tears
and sadness—it's sometimes easier to let
things slide than to stop everything and
put extra energy into disciplining.
Give me the strength and wisdom to
do what is right and not skirt over
disobedience when it arises. Help me
to keep love the driving motivator
for expecting good behavior and
developing strong character.
In Christ I pray.
AMEN.

THEY ARE
NEVER ALONE

Do not let [My commands] leave your heart
for the rest of your life. But teach them to
your children and to your grandchildren.

DEUTERONOMY 4:9 NLV

Lord, I want my children to know You and
Your promises. I want them to stand firm
in their faith and walk with integrity and
might. At some point they will probably
encounter kids who bully, unjust teachers
that treat them unfairly, and rejection from
other students. Help me to teach them
about the power and strength they have
when they call on You and that they are
never alone. Ever. Help me to prepare
them for what You know they'll face.
In Your name I trust.

AMEN.

DEALING WITH DEFIANCE

It's a school of hard knocks for those who leave God's path, a dead-end street for those who hate God's rules.
PROVERBS 15:10 THE MESSAGE

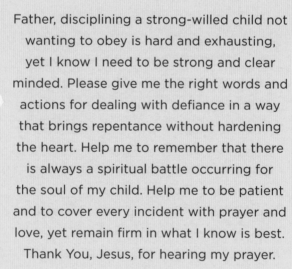

Father, disciplining a strong-willed child not wanting to obey is hard and exhausting, yet I know I need to be strong and clear minded. Please give me the right words and actions for dealing with defiance in a way that brings repentance without hardening the heart. Help me to remember that there is always a spiritual battle occurring for the soul of my child. Help me to be patient and to cover every incident with prayer and love, yet remain firm in what I know is best. Thank You, Jesus, for hearing my prayer.
AMEN.

BEING ALL THINGS

I [Paul] have become all things to all people, so that I may by every possible means save some.
I CORINTHIANS 9:22

Lord, this is what I feel like I have to do every day as a mother: be all things to each member of my family. Wife, mother, counselor, physician, valet, teacher, chef... The list seems endless. Give me grace. Give me strength. Give me Your special touch so that I am able to do them well and, at the end of the day, my family will see You and I can rest in fulfillment. That is my prayer lifted in Your sweet name.
AMEN.

ASK FOR
A MIRACLE

*Now to Him who is able to do above and
beyond all that we ask or think according to
the power that works in us.*

EPHESIANS 3:20

Father, I need a miracle today. Yet it seems I need
a miracle every day—for strength not to get swept
away by the ever-evolving items on my to-do list.
Then there's my constant wondering how all the
bills will get paid. Then there are the lists of needs
my children have. And the future—am I doing
enough to prepare for their future?! Lord, I need
help! Bring me back to the clear reminder that
You have me covered. Rein in my imagination so
it's back to the reality that You are great and able
to do above and beyond all that I ask or think.
All for Your glory.

AMEN.

FOLLOWING HIM
CAN BE HARD

"I'll go with You, wherever,"
[the man] said. Jesus was curt:
"Are you ready to rough it?
We're not staying in the
best inns, you know."
LUKE 9:57-58 THE MESSAGE

Lord, this is a good reminder that following
You isn't always easy. It requires getting
out of my comfort zone and going where
You lead, even when surroundings aren't
perfect or pleasant. Give me the courage
and strength I need to do what You ask and
be where You want me to be with faith
and trust that doesn't waver.
All glory to You.
AMEN.

WALK WORTHY

*Walk worthy of the Lord, fully pleasing
to Him: bearing fruit in every good work
and growing in the knowledge of God,
being strengthened with all power,
according to His glorious might.*

COLOSSIANS 1:10-11

Lord, it is my prayer today that I walk
worthy of You. I want to please You—
as a woman, a mom, a disciple. The more
I learn and the closer I grow toward You,
I am assured of Your power in me to rise to
whatever task comes today. Knowing that
forgiveness is there for the times I slip, and
grace awaits when I fall brings such relief
and love and thanksgiving. Help me to
extend the same grace and forgiveness.
In Your great name.

AMEN.

SEND UP
YOUR PRAYERS

But you, LORD, don't be far away.
My strength, come quickly to help me.
PSALM 22:19

Lord, thank You for always being with
me. You hem me in and keep me by Your
side. I'm glad I don't have to know all
the answers to my daily questions about
parenting because You do. You are with me
to lead and to guide. You help me through
confusing and draining days and bless me
with fun and joyous ones. Remind me to
take deep breaths and send up prayers to
You for help as many times as I need—
You aren't counting!
Thank You, Jesus.
AMEN.

HE PROTECTS

The LORD is my strength and my shield;
my heart trusts in Him, and I am helped.
Therefore my heart celebrates,
and I give thanks to Him with my song.
PSALM 28:7

Lord, I cannot tell You what relief I have
knowing I can trust You in all things.
The more I trust in You, the more
confidence and peace and energy I have.
You are my family's Protector—You guard
us from unwanted forces and shield us from
the enemy's attacks from all sides.
Thank You for how empowered this makes
me feel, knowing You are with us and for us.
In Your Son's name.
AMEN.

CUT THE CORDS

*Jesus replied, "No one who puts a hand
to the plow and looks back is fit for
service in the kingdom of God."*

LUKE 9:62 NIV

Lord, help me not to look back at hurtful
and painful times I've had. Give me the
strength and trust I need to look forward
to the new and good things You have in
store. Help me to cut the cords that keep
me stuck in the past so I can move into
the next steps You have for me with a free
and clear heart. Help me to hold on to the
healing You give and the joy that is mine
through You. In Your sweet name I pray.

AMEN.

HIS POWER
IS YOURS

"I am not able to," Joseph answered
Pharaoh. "It is God who will give
Pharaoh a favorable answer."
GENESIS 41:16

Father, this is a wonderful reminder that
there isn't much at all I can do on my own
strength and power, yet anything is mine to
do in Yours. Please help me keep my sights
on this truth today. Help me stay fixed on
Your power that is in me for accomplishing
the work You've put before me.
I am not able, but You are.
All praise be to You.
AMEN.

STRENGTH FOR EACH DAY

Now to Him who is able to establish and strengthen you [in the faith] according to my gospel and the preaching of Jesus Christ.

ROMANS 16:25 AMP

Father, I need strength and ask You to establish Yours within me. I need it every day to keep up with the pace of life, with my family's needs, and for my own good. I trust You to provide the energy and endurance I'll need for whatever this day brings. You are my provider, and You provide abundantly. I am so grateful I can call on You at any moment for help, no matter how small the need.
Blessed be Your name.

AMEN.

APRIL

PATIENCE

WHAT IS TRULY IMPORTANT

God is the One who makes us patient and
cheerful. I pray that He will help you
live at peace with each other,
as you follow Christ.

ROMANS 15:5 CEV

Father, You know and I know that patience
is not one of my best virtues. I want to be
patient, especially with my children,
but I often lose it more than I exercise it.
Please help me today to slow down and
focus on what is truly important, and that
is love—not just accomplishing a task
or sticking to an agenda.
I need Your grace and help today.
In Jesus' name.

AMEN.

PATIENCE AND TRUST

Wait for the Lord; be strong,
and let your heart be courageous.
Wait for the Lord.

PSALM 27:14

Lord, it's hard to wait—on just about
anything! It takes patience and trust
combined, and I so often hold on to both by
a thread. But I know that if I want to teach
my child how to wait with patience, I must
be the example of what that looks like—
by fully embracing my trust in You.
Help me, Lord. Help me to be and do what
I want passed on to my family.
All glory to You.

AMEN.

PATIENCE IS A FRUIT

The fruit of the Spirit is love, joy, peace, patience, kindness, goodness, faithfulness, gentleness, and self-control.

GALATIANS 5:22-23

Father, when I lean on Your Spirit
for guidance, timing, conviction,
direction—everything!—I have more
contentment and patience in my very being.
That's because Your ways are so different
and less burdensome than the daily
pressures I put on myself in this fast pace of
living. Help me to display all of the fruit of
Your Spirit, which comes from leaning
on You, but especially help me
to have patience.
To You, Jesus, I pray.
AMEN.

GET TO THE ROOT

Those with good sense are slow to anger.
PROVERBS 19:11 NRSV

Lord, it seems the smallest things set me off so quickly—and I don't want to live that way. What is it, Lord? Help me to look deeper and see what the root cause of my impatience and snappy responses are so I can work through it. Whether it be unforgiveness, resentment, or just being overworked and underappreciated, help me to see what it is so I can address it and not let it control me so negatively. I want to be controlled by Your gentle and loving Spirit, and nothing else. Help me, Jesus.

AMEN.

BEARING IN LOVE

I, the prisoner in the Lord, urge you to live
worthy of the calling you have received, with
all humility and gentleness, with patience,
bearing with one another in love.
EPHESIANS 4:1-2

Father, I think walking in humility and
gentleness is key to bearing with one
another in love. But I often don't bear in
love—it's usually in hurried quips. I want to
be humble and gentle and patient with my
family. I want my children to learn this as
well. Please help me to stop and breathe
and remember that love is what matters
most. Help me to cover others with
love the way You cover me.
In Your name I pray.
AMEN.

WALK IN HIS GRACE

God has been very kind to you,
and He has been patient with you.
God has been waiting for you to change.
ROMANS 2:4 ICB

O Lord, You have been very kind to me.
And patient. It's taken years to change old
habits—some still creep back into my life,
and yet You continue to shower Your love
on me. Help me to remember the patience
I've received so I will, in turn, have patience
with my growing kids. Help me to have
patience with myself! Help me to remove
the high expectations I place on my
own life and, instead, walk in the
blessing of Your grace.
All praise to You.
AMEN.

SOME GOOD EXAMPLES

Follow the example of the prophets who spoke for the Lord. They suffered many hard things, but they were patient.

JAMES 5:10 NCV

Lord, life can be so challenging and hard—it takes patience and endurance to make it through some of the long, dark valleys. But it's hard to have patience while living at such a fast pace. With so many conveniences and technologies that provide quick results, having to slowly work through trials feels foreign. I'm grateful for the greats in the Bible and their testimonies of character and undying hope in You. Their examples instill a challenge in me to grow my faith and remain patient in spite of affliction. All glory to You, Jesus.

AMEN.

JESUS WAITED

The light from the sun was gone—and
suddenly the thick veil hanging in the
Temple split apart. Then Jesus shouted,
"Father, I commit My spirit to You,"
and with those words He died.
LUKE 23:45–46 TLB

Lord Jesus, You didn't run away in a panic.
You didn't try to get Your death over with
quickly. You endured. You waited for Your
Father's perfect timing. You were patient
to let circumstances occur that would lead
up to the very miracle of Your resurrection.
Oh, please, forgive me for trying to hurry
up anything ahead of You. Help me to have
patience and accept the timing You want
me to have for Your glory, not my own.
In Jesus' great name.
AMEN.

SEEK UNDERSTANDING

A patient person shows great understanding, but a quick-tempered one promotes foolishness.

PROVERBS 14:29

Father, help me to seek and to find greater understanding...the next time my teenager looks away and clams up; the next time my middle schooler outright disobeys; the next time my normally sweet and quiet girl lashes out and throws a tantrum. Help me to see through outward rebellion and into what is really wrong. And give me the patience and love I need to bring healing and structure, calm and assurance. Thank You, Lord, for hearing my prayer.

AMEN.

HE ROSE

*"Go find My brothers and tell them that I
ascend to My Father and your Father,
My God and your God." Mary Magdalene
found the disciples and told them,
"I have seen the Lord!"*

JOHN 20:17-18 TLB

Lord Jesus, Your resurrection is the miracle
that sets You apart from any other religion.
It's the crux of the Christian faith. I am so
grateful for Your sacrifice and the promise of
eternal life I have in You. Since You died for
me, since You bless me with Your resurrection
and Spirit, I must trust in You through all of
my circumstances. I want my life to be a
sacrifice for Your kingdom and glory.
In Your glorious name.
AMEN.

WALK WORTHY

Walk worthy of the Lord, fully pleasing to Him: bearing fruit...so that you may have great endurance and patience.

COLOSSIANS 1:10-11

Father, I hope I am walking worthy of my calling as a mother. I try my very best, and I know I couldn't do all I do without Your help. I am also very thankful for the patience You have with me as I trek this journey of mine. I know I haven't even scratched the surface of all there is to learn, let alone all there is to teach and instill in my children. You are my source of life and hope for each new day. All worship and praise to You.

AMEN.

THE BIBLE
HAS THE ANSWERS

*Preach the Word; be ready in season and out
of season; rebuke, correct, and encourage
with great patience and teaching.*

II TIMOTHY 4:2

O Lord, I'm so thankful for Your Word.
It is blessed truth in a world that is so full
of lies. I want to use Your instruction as the
foundation and backdrop for decisions I
have to make and for challenging my family
to learn its treasures too. I'm grateful and
relieved to know that every answer to my
problems is found in the Bible. Help me now
to make time to read it every day.
In Jesus' name.

AMEN.

HOPE IN HIM

If we hope for what we do not see,
we eagerly wait for it with patience.

ROMANS 8:25

Father, I often do not see how I'm going to accomplish all there is to do, but my hope is in You for help. I do not see where the resources will come from to pay all of the bills, but my hope is in You to provide. I do not see what the future holds for my child or even for myself, but my hope is in the truth that You have a plan, and You are for us. All praise and glory to You this day.

AMEN.

ON GUARD
WITH PATIENCE

Patience is better than power,
and controlling one's emotions,
than capturing a city.
PROVERBS 16:32

O Lord, how I need patience so I don't
lose control of my attitudes and emotions.
I don't want impatience or a quick temper
to be my norm. I pray You will help me to
slow down and say a prayer the next time
I'm tempted to let a short fuse take over.
Please help me to be calm and take godly
control that pleases You the next time the
kids argue or disobey. Help me to be on
guard and ready to exercise Your
love and patience.
In the power of Your Spirit I pray.
AMEN.

CONTROLLING YOUR TONGUE

A person takes joy in giving an answer;
and a timely word—how good that is!
PROVERBS 15:23

Father, controlling my tongue begins with
controlling my thoughts. Help me to take
my thoughts captive to this verse today.
May my thoughts come from a deeper
longing to understand mercy and grace,
compassion and love. Put a guard over my
mouth and give me grace to say only
those things You would have me say.
In Your name I pray.
AMEN.

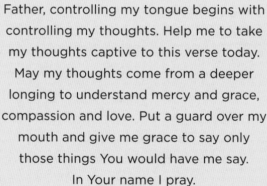

IN HIS TIME

After waiting patiently,
Abraham obtained the promise.
HEBREWS 6:15

Lord, You have given me dreams and
desires that I'm just not able to pursue or
fulfill right now. Being a mom, caring for my
family, working to do all I can to help make
ends meet is so demanding of my time and
energy. Please give me patience and strong
hope that soon I will have opportunities to
pursue the other dreams You've given me.
All in Your good and perfect time.
I love You, Lord.
AMEN.

FINDING GOOD IN THE ROADBLOCKS

The human mind may devise many plans,
but it is the purpose of the
LORD that will be established.

PROVERBS 19:21 NRSV

Father, I get so impatient and anxious
when things don't work out as planned.
I confess I forget that You are always
working out Your purpose in my life and
my family. Instead of getting stressed,
I want to see hiccups or roadblocks as
Your way of redirecting each day and not
necessarily as a problem. I want to take
these more in stride rather than take them
on as a challenge. Help me to breathe and
remember that You are in control.
All praise to You.
AMEN.

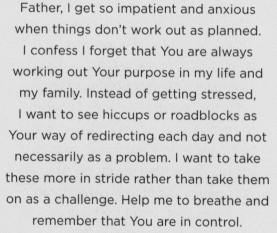

WAIT ON HIS TIMING

We wait for the LORD;
He is our help and shield.
PSALM 33:20

Father, sometimes it's really hard to wait
on You. It seems the longer my children see
a prayer not yet answered, I want to jump
in and take over. The older I get and the
longer I wait for my dreams to become
a reality, the more restless I feel.
Please help me—help my family—
to trust in Your timing and Your ways.
Shield me from the temptation to rush
ahead of You. Help me be the example
of patience and faith my children
need to learn for themselves.
In Jesus I pray.
AMEN.

PURPOSE IN PAIN

If we are afflicted, it is for your comfort and salvation. If we are comforted, it is for your comfort, which produces in you patient endurance of the same sufferings that we suffer.

II CORINTHIANS 1:6

Father, affliction in my life certainly takes its toll, but to see it in my child's life is really hard. I want so much to protect and guard from hurt and pain, yet it's impossible to shelter an innocent mind and heart from every injury. Help me to comfort and console and to remember that You build patience and endurance through painful trials. Both are very needed for living on this earth—they are not to be endured in vain. Thank You, Jesus.

AMEN.

UNDERSTANDING BRINGS PATIENCE

I pursue the way of Your commands,
for You broaden my understanding.

PSALM 119:32

Lord, I love how You give understanding in certain situations and at times when I really need it. Having understanding helps me to have patience with Your time line and with Your desired outcomes—and with other people who often try my patience! Help me to keep You in the forefront of each trying situation I face—that is, Your wisdom, Your love, and Your saving grace as the catalyst for my responses. Thank You for Your Word and the understanding it brings. Bless Your holy name.

AMEN.

WALK IN GRACE

We have all received grace upon grace from His fullness, for the law was given through Moses; grace and truth came through Jesus Christ.

JOHN 1:16–17

Lord, since I am covered by Your grace, why do I continually beat myself up for the mistakes I make? Why am I so hard on myself for losing patience with my children and with myself? It's as though I condemn myself for things You don't even condemn me for. Please help me to walk in freedom from condemnation and in the fullness of Your grace and love. And help me to extend the same to my family. Thank You for hearing my prayer.

AMEN.

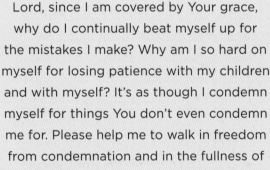

JUST BE PRESENT

You will fill me with
gladness in Your presence.
ACTS 2:28

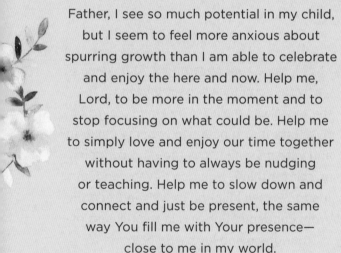

Father, I see so much potential in my child,
but I seem to feel more anxious about
spurring growth than I am able to celebrate
and enjoy the here and now. Help me,
Lord, to be more in the moment and to
stop focusing on what could be. Help me
to simply love and enjoy our time together
without having to always be nudging
or teaching. Help me to slow down and
connect and just be present, the same
way You fill me with Your presence—
close to me in my world.
I love You, Lord.
AMEN.

HE NEVER
GIVES UP

All that He does is splendid and majestic;
His righteousness endures forever....
The LORD is gracious and compassionate.

PSALM 111:3-4

Lord, Your blessings, Your promises—
they are so wonderful and too many to count. It
means a lot to me that Your righteousness doesn't
end—You don't get impatient and cut Yourself off
because You've waited long enough for humankind
to come around to You. You endure—forever.
Help me...help me to endure through trials and
challenges. Help me not to give up on others or on
myself.
Help me to take on Your qualities of grace and
compassion toward others,
because I need them too.

AMEN.

RESPOND
WITH PATIENCE

Better a patient person than a
warrior, one with self-control
than one who takes a city.
PROVERBS 16:32 NIV

O Lord, I have a full day today, and I pray
for You to guard my time and energy.
Help me remember that I'm only so much
in control—You are ultimately the One who
orchestrates how events play out.
If something doesn't go according to plan,
help me control my responses with patience
and remember that You are present.
You are with me to help. Help me to
carry Your Spirit of love throughout
the day no matter what.
In Your grace I pray.
AMEN.

THE TESTING OF FAITH

Consider it a great joy...sisters,
whenever you experience various trials,
because you know that the testing of your
faith produces endurance.

JAMES 1:2-3

Father, I can see that You want me to
develop patience and endurance the same
way I want my children to. And some days
it's hard—I don't think I can endure any more
testing. My faith seems peaked out.
But I hold on to hope. I want to find Your
joy in my trials. I want to endure to the
next mountaintop to be scaled.
You are an amazing God,
and I lift my trust and praise to You.

AMEN.

THE BIGGER PICTURE IN VIEW

Who is like the LORD our God—the One enthroned on high, who stoops down to look on the heavens and the earth?

PSALM 113:5-6

Father, I get so focused on each activity in my day, my fuse feels as short as the very moment I'm focused on. Help me to stop and step back. Help me to keep the bigger picture of life in view so the present moment won't feel so urgent. In the scheme of a lifetime, most upsetting things are so small, they don't deserve the energy I give them. You've got a bigger picture and bigger plan than I see and know about. I want to trust You more and rest in that plan. In the power of Your name, I pray.

AMEN.

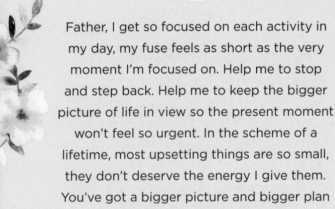

GROWTH, ONE DAY AT A TIME

Like newborn babies,
crave pure spiritual milk,
so that by it you may grow up
in your salvation.

I PETER 2:2 NIV

Lord, I want so much to be more mature
in my faith, but I feel like whenever I make
any progress, something happens and I
take two steps backward. It's challenging
to find time to be still, to study my Bible,
and to be quiet in prayer. I'm so grateful for
Your patience and loving-kindness to me.
Now help me to have patience with myself.
I know that life happens one day at a time,
and my growth will too. Give me an open
heart and mind for what You would teach
me today. In Your grace I pray.

AMEN.

PATIENCE IN PROGRESS

We teach in a spirit of profound common sense so that we can bring each person to maturity. To be mature is to be basic. Christ!
COLOSSIANS 1:28 THE MESSAGE

Father, I see so much potential in my child that isn't yet being realized. I wonder what I could do better to help along more growth—sometimes I want to see progress come faster than it is. Please give me patience as I steer and guide, teach and encourage both directly and from the sidelines. It's a balance I couldn't achieve without Your help. Thank You, Lord.

AMEN.

REST IN FAITH

*As for me, I am poor and needy; come
quickly to me, O God. You are my help and
my deliverer; L*ORD*, do not delay.*

PSALM 70:5 NIV

Lord, I keep praying to You for help in
certain ways, but I've not heard from You.
I am waiting, and rather impatiently.
Help me to take a deep breath and trust
You. Help me remember Your faithfulness
in the past and believe You will send an
answer in Your perfect time. Give me the
patience that comes with having faith.
In Your sweet name.

AMEN.

UNTIL THAT DAY

Sisters, be patient until the Lord's coming.
See how the farmer waits for the precious
fruit of the earth and is patient with it until
it receives the early and the late rains.

JAMES 5:7

Lord, I often lose sight of the bigger
picture of my Christian walk: we are all
waiting for Your return. You are coming
back to us, we just don't know when.
Help me to remember this perspective the
next time I get so focused on minute daily
things. In the bigger scheme of my life,
I am waiting for You. Until that day comes,
I want to be found expectant and wholly
devoted to sharing the gospel message and
to spreading Your love. Until that day.

AMEN.

MAY

TRUST

TRUST IN THE LORD

Trust in the LORD with all your heart,
and do not rely on your own understanding;
in all your ways know Him, and He
will make your paths straight.

PROVERBS 3:5-6

Father, it's hard to turn off my thoughts
about how to work through problems I'm
facing. I have so many questions about how
to teach, how to discipline, how to nurture,
and how to explain painful situations to my
child. I know my intellect can only think so
far and it can be deceiving. At some point I
must release the unknowns to You and trust
You with all my heart that You'll show me
step by step what to do and when.
I cast my cares on You now and
entrust them to You with all my heart.

AMEN.

A HEART
THAT BELIEVES

The Lord said to Moses...
"How long will they not believe in Me,
despite all the [miraculous] signs which
I have performed among them?"
NUMBERS 14:11 AMP

O Lord, I confess I am guilty of this same
thing: not trusting in You after You've
clearly worked wonders in my life.
You'd think that because of the goodness
You've shown, I wouldn't hesitate at all to
trust in You when circumstances around
me are unclear. Please forgive me and help
me now to ward off any doubt that comes
to mind. You have been faithful before,
and I believe You will continue to bless and
provide in Your perfect way and time.
In Jesus' name.
AMEN.

BE A LOYAL FOLLOWER

Those who know Your name trust in You because You have not abandoned those who seek You, LORD.

PSALM 9:10

Father, this is so true. Since following You, I cannot think of a time You ever left me on my own. But I can think of times I've abandoned You in order to follow my own heart—and I live with the regret. But I am stayed on You now. I need You, I trust You with my life and how You want to use it. Please continue to help and guide me, and give me courage to go where You lead. I want to trust You as the greats in the Bible did thousands of years ago. I pray in the heart and Spirit of Jesus.

AMEN.

TRUST IS THE ONLY ANSWER

You did not trust the LORD your God,
who went before you on the journey to
seek out a place for you to camp.

DEUTERONOMY 1:32-33

O Lord, this is so convicting because I do
the same thing: in spite of all the ways
You've provided and blessed me and my
family, I still lack trust. Please forgive me.
My focus on my problems overshadows my
focus on Your faithfulness, and I'm sorry.
I look to You now and remember...
I remember the kindness You have shown
and the answers to prayers—sometimes
even greater than I ever thought possible.
You are a good, good God, and I love You.

AMEN.

FRAGILE TRUST

His source of confidence is fragile; what he trusts in is a spider's web. He leans on his web, but it doesn't stand firm. He grabs it, but it does not hold up.

JOB 8:14-15

Father, I shudder to think of all the things this world tells my children to put their trust in. I feel an urgency to protect them and sometimes even isolate them from the influences that are all around.
I pray for their minds to see and want You— to see that You are the only source that is completely trustworthy. Help me to be the best example for them to follow.
In Your great name.

AMEN.

TRUST IN
HIS STRENGTH

Those who trust in the LORD will find new
strength. They will soar high on wings like
eagles. They will run and not grow
weary. They will walk and not faint.
ISAIAH 40:31 NLT

Father, sometimes life can be so
exhausting and overwhelming,
I continuously return to the humble state
that I cannot bear the weight and pressure
alone. You have been a constant source of
strength and refreshment as I place my full
and committed trust in You for help.
I believe in my heart that You won't give me
more than I can handle and that You will
provide new power and vigor to overcome
any weakness or temptation to give up.
In Your great and glorious name.
AMEN.

TRUST HIS WORD

The instruction of the LORD is perfect,
renewing one's life; the testimony of
the LORD is trustworthy, making the
inexperienced wise.

PSALM 19:7

Lord, I believe Your Word is truth.
Each story You tell, each pledge of
assurance breathes new life in me in ways I
cannot explain except that You are present.
You are there in the pages calling me to
You. The knowledge I gain through the
chapters is priceless, as are the stories of
faith that inspire and help me to know how
to live. Your faithfulness reads through
centuries of promises fulfilled, including
that of a Savior—the One who died on my
behalf so I can spend eternity with You.
All praise be to You, Father God.

AMEN.

COMPLETE TRUST

Immediately the father cried out,
"I do believe! Help me to believe more!"
MARK 9:24 NCV

Father, oh how I can relate to this man's
struggle with unbelief, especially when
it comes to You healing his child. It's a
helpless feeling to see a child suffer and
there's nothing you can do for them.
I want to believe in You to the point that
there is no hesitation on my part when it
comes to trusting You with my children's
lives. The way a toddler trustingly jumps to
her father in a pool, I want the same pure
and simple belief that You are there with
arms open wide and that You are in control.
In Jesus' name.
AMEN.

NOTHING TO FEAR

Behold, God is my salvation; I will trust, and will not be afraid; for the LORD GOD is my strength and my song, and He has become my salvation.

ISAIAH 12:2 ESV

Lord, You are my salvation and my hope at all times. You've delivered a way— through Your Son, Jesus—for me to enter into Your presence of grace, now and for eternity. The weight and burden of my sins are lifted, and I can sing a new song of love to You. Because of Your faithfulness, I can trust in You with my whole heart and being. I have nothing to fear on this earth— help me to walk in that certainty today. All praise and glory to You.

AMEN.

DEPEND ON
HIM ONLY

You will keep the mind that is
dependent on You in perfect peace,
for it is trusting in You.
ISAIAH 26:3

Lord, I can tell I've been focusing on
my circumstances because I feel anxious
and stressed. Help me to block out all the
"what-ifs" and turn my thoughts to the
power I possess through You. You fill my
heart with hope and my body with peace
and rest. No one and no thing can compare
to the greatness of You, so today,
once again, I place my trust in You.
Thank You for being my refuge and
constant source of strength.
In Jesus' name.
AMEN.

FLOURISHING TRUST

Anyone trusting in his riches will fall,
but the righteous will flourish like foliage.
PROVERBS 11:28

Father, society says a full bank account,
a fancy car, a beautiful home and, children
to fill it means a happy and fulfilling life.
These are all nice things to have, but
nothing brings complete security but You.
Knowing You, living for You, carrying out
Your purposes, walking and being led by
Your Spirit—this is where my trust will
remain because You promise to complete
what You have started in my life. I love and
trust You today, tomorrow, and always.
All glory to You.
AMEN.

STOP TRUSTING YOURSELF

We felt sure that we were going to die.
But this [horrible suffering] made us stop
trusting in ourselves and start trusting God,
who raises the dead to life.
II CORINTHIANS 1:9 CEV

Father, because Jesus sacrificed Himself on my behalf, I am sealed with the promise of spending eternity with You. This means I no longer have to fear death—I can trust You for eternal life. What relief and joy this brings! I no longer walk in fear because my very life is in Your hands. Help me to teach this truth to my children—that we can all be filled with the confidence of Your presence and power, knowing our future is secure. Thank You, Jesus, for Your gift of sacrifice.

AMEN.

TRUST IN GOD'S WISDOM

A man is a fool to trust himself!
But those who use God's wisdom are safe.

PROVERBS 28:26 TLB

Lord, not only do I not trust myself,
I ask that You save me from myself! I am
my own worst enemy and shudder to think
of the times I thought I knew the answers
to my problems, only to find bigger messes
in the end. I look to You now and confess
Your ways are best. I want Your power, Your
promises, and Your presence to be my help.
I don't always understand Your ways, but I
trust that You have only my and my family's
best interests and Your great glory in mind.
I'm so thankful for Your patient love.

AMEN.

TRUST IN HIS DELIVERANCE

When Daniel was brought up from the den,
he was found to be unharmed,
for he trusted in his God.

DANIEL 6:23

Father, if Daniel can trust You to deliver him from a den of hungry lions, I can trust You to be with me in the circumstances I face today. But even more, help me to teach this story of faith and commitment to my kids. Help me to help them to see past the immediate details of what they face, and trust that You see the bigger picture of their lives. You know how best to arrange circumstances so that Your presence is evident to them. I trust You to lead, guide, and deliver us all to receive blessing, and that You will receive glory.

AMEN.

TRUST IN HIS PROTECTION

*The fear of mankind is a snare, but the one
who trusts in the L ORD is protected.*

PROVERBS 29:25

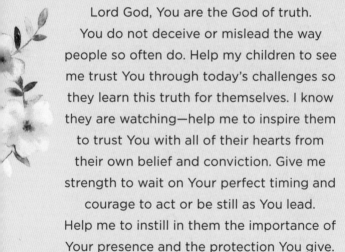

Lord God, You are the God of truth.
You do not deceive or mislead the way
people so often do. Help my children to see
me trust You through today's challenges so
they learn this truth for themselves. I know
they are watching—help me to inspire them
to trust You with all of their hearts from
their own belief and conviction. Give me
strength to wait on Your perfect timing and
courage to act or be still as You lead.
Help me to instill in them the importance of
Your presence and the protection You give.
All praise be to You.

AMEN.

TRUST HIS
SAVING GRACE

This saying is trustworthy and deserving
of full acceptance: "Christ Jesus came
into the world to save sinners."

I TIMOTHY 1:15

O Lord, my heart is filled with sweet
relief to know that You came to save—
me, my children, and everyone!
Your mercies are new every morning,
and Your faithfulness is great.
Sometimes the stress of the day distracts
me from these truths. Help me to keep this
gift in the forefront of my mind in spite of
all the busy schedules and activities. You
proved Your love for us all through Your
death, therefore, how can I not trust
You completely with all of our lives?
In Your precious name I pray.

AMEN.

TRUST IN TRUE LIFE

This saying is trustworthy: For if we died with Him, we will also live with Him.
II TIMOTHY 2:11

Father, the enemy is cunning and deceptive at making my "self" look great on the throne of my life. But I want to see through the lies and ask Your heart to take supreme residence in mine. I want to live for You and be used to complete Your purposes for me as a mother and whatever else You want to do with my life. I would rather spend one day in Your courts and experience true fullness of life than spend a thousand elsewhere. I want to die to my own selfish ways and trust in the newness of life that You give. All glory to You, my loving Savior.
AMEN.

TRUST IN
HIS PROMISES

*All Scripture is God-breathed
and is useful for teaching...and training
in righteousness, so that the servant of
God may be thoroughly equipped
for every good work.*

II TIMOTHY 3:16-17 NIV

Father, the gift of Your Word is the finest of
treasures and greatest of sources for arming
us with wisdom and truth in a chaotic world.
Every word can be trusted for helping; every
story can be used as a means of inspiration
for spurring me on as I learn and teach my
child about You. I love reading from Your
heart about how to live so that we can all
experience the greatest communion and
blessing with You each moment throughout
our day. In Your holy name.

AMEN.

THE VOICE OF TRUTH

While [Peter] was still speaking...
a voice from the cloud said:
"This is My beloved Son, with whom I
am well-pleased. Listen to Him!"
MATTHEW 17:5

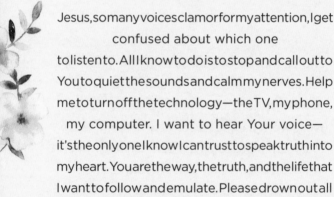

Jesus, so many voices clamor for my attention, I get confused about which one to listen to. All I know to do is to stop and call out to You to quiet the sounds and calm my nerves. Help me to turn off the technology—the TV, my phone, my computer. I want to hear Your voice—it's the only one I know I can trust to speak truth into my heart. You are the way, the truth, and the life that I want to follow and emulate. Please drown out all other noises so that Your voice is unmistakable. All thanks and praise to You.

AMEN.

GUARD
YOUR HEART

Guard your heart above all else,
for it is the source of life.

PROVERBS 4:23

Dear Lord, trusting You means freedom for
my soul. It creates a seal of armor around my
heart that keeps me from harm and lets me
dance in the protection of Your presence.
Please stop the enemy's attempts to injure my
heart and put negative thoughts in my mind.
Instead, guard them both with Your coat of
love and life. I want to live and run freely in full
and complete trust in You, and I know I can
when You are watching over me.
Thank You for Your shelter and care.
In Jesus' sweet name.

AMEN.

TRUST IN HIS FAITHFULNESS

I have trusted in Your faithful love;
my heart will rejoice in Your deliverance.
I will sing to the Lord because He has
treated me generously.

PSALM 13:5-6

Father, You have blessed my life so
abundantly; You have surrounded me
with favor in more ways than I can count.
When I think on times You've delivered me
from the messes I've made, the falls I've
encountered—each time You were there to
pick me up and cover me with Your grace.
You have poured out to me the promises
of Your Word and Your faithfulness to fulfill
them. I am ever so grateful for Your love—
a love I trust to sustain my very life.

AMEN.

TRUST THAT SAFEGUARDS

You are my rock and my fortress;
You lead and guide me for Your name's sake.
You will free me from the net
that is secretly set for me.

PSALM 31:3-4

Father, each moment throughout my day,
the enemy tries to get my focus off You and
cause me to stress over the demands I'm
facing. Please safeguard my attention to
keep You at the center of everything—
my words, my thoughts, my work,
and my actions. I claim the confidence that
is mine when I look to You as my Rock of
life, and I trust in the secure foundation You
provide. Please bless this day to be without
wavering or second-guessing as I keep
my eyes fixed on You.

AMEN.

TRUST IN
HIS PROVISION

He waters the mountains from His palace....
He causes grass to grow for the livestock
and provides crops for man to cultivate...
and bread that sustains human hearts.

PSALM 104:13–15

Father, Your provision is all around—
it is abundant beyond what I deserve.
You've provided in the past, and I trust You
will now. The end-of-school-year activities,
the yearbook, the summer programs to
register for—the "needs" list doesn't ever
seem to get shorter, but longer.
But Your faithfulness has been true since
the beginning of time, and it is obvious
now. I trust You for Your provision
today and the next.
All thanks be to Jesus.
AMEN.

TRUST HIS LEADING

*Test me, L*ORD*, and try me; examine*
my heart and mind. For Your faithful
love guides me, and I live by Your truth.
PSALM 26:2-3

Father, please do examine my heart and
let me know if there is anything—thought,
word, or attitude—that is offensive to You.
The enemy is so subtle at fooling me into
doing things that seem okay yet are not
quite in line with Your Word. I want to be
sensitive to Your leading and the nudges
You give when I've said or done something
that isn't in harmony with Your ways.
I want to trust in Your faithful love alone.
AMEN.

TRUST IN
HIS WAYS

I always let the Lord guide me.
Because He is at my right hand,
I will not be shaken.

PSALM 16:8

Lord, I cannot count the number of nights
I've spent lying awake thinking on the past
day's events. I wonder how I could have
responded to challenges differently for
better outcomes. But then I remember that
all I can do is learn from my mistakes and
continue to trust Your ways, not my own.
Knowing You are with me and in control of
all things calms my spirit and blesses me
with peace like no other, and I am thankful.
In Jesus' name.

AMEN.

TRUST HIM WHEN YOU TITHE

*"Bring the full tenth into
the storehouse.... Test Me in this way,"
says the LORD of Armies.*
MALACHI 3:10

Father, when it comes to tithing, I want to give cheerfully, yet I worry I won't have enough left to do all the things I want or need to do. Help me to hear your voice and to follow your lead. Help me to be generous and use me to meet the needs of those around me so that You will be glorified and honored. Show me how to give, what to give, and when to give it. It's all yours, God. Open my eyes to how to best use it.
In Jesus' name.
AMEN.

TRUST HIS WAYS

My thoughts are not your thoughts,
and your ways are not My ways.
ISAIAH 55:8

Lord, I get confused when I think I
should do one thing, yet You lead me to
do something that doesn't make sense.
These are the times when I have to choose
whom I am going to serve—You or myself.
I guess it boils down to whether or not I
trust You enough with the outcome and
believe it will be for my best interest and
for Your glory. Please forgive my hesitation
at times. My life is not my own—Your
goodness and splendor are the goal.
In Your name I place my trust.
AMEN.

TRUST THAT
HE SEES

Do not fret (whine, agonize) because of him
who prospers in his way, because of the man
who carries out wicked schemes.

PSALM 37:7 AMP

Father, it's hard to watch someone who
is arrogant prosper in whatever they do,
while I seem to be overlooked. Help me
to believe with confidence that You see
all things, and You know the intent of
everyone's heartsand that my reward will
come in its time. You are in control and I am
right where You want me. Help me not to
compare my life with another's but learn to
have patience as I draw from the peace
You put in my heart.
All praise and glory to Your name.

AMEN.

TRUST HIM
TO VICTORY

The Rock—His work is perfect;
all His ways are just. A faithful God...
He is righteous and true.
DEUTERONOMY 32:4

Father, I'm in a trial that is testing my faith,
and the enemy keeps whispering for me to
give up. But I love You and know You love
me. I have to believe You are with me now
orchestrating events that will work for my
good. I trust You to guide my steps and
lead me to victory, no matter how
thick the battle gets. I trust You to protect
my heart and guard my thoughts so that
Your strength and power will rule.
In the power of Jesus in me I pray.
AMEN.

TRUST HIM WITH FUTURE GENERATIONS

Start a youth out on his way; even when he grows old he will not depart from it.

PROVERBS 22:6

Lord, I think of our youth today and how so many who've grown up in church don't stay in church after they've left home. I pray Your voice will always call to them, including my own children: that the longings of this world will not satisfy but leave them empty and wanting more of You. I entrust them to You to have Your way so that their eyes would be enlightened to Your truth over the lies and false testimonies that lure them away from Your house. Help them to see that trust in You is the only way toward life and fulfillment. In Jesus' name.

AMEN.

TRUST HIM TO THE FINISH LINE

Let us run with endurance the race that lies before us, keeping our eyes on Jesus, the source and perfecter of our faith.

HEBREWS 12:1-2

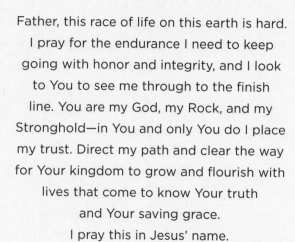

Father, this race of life on this earth is hard. I pray for the endurance I need to keep going with honor and integrity, and I look to You to see me through to the finish line. You are my God, my Rock, and my Stronghold—in You and only You do I place my trust. Direct my path and clear the way for Your kingdom to grow and flourish with lives that come to know Your truth and Your saving grace. I pray this in Jesus' name.

AMEN.

JUNE

COURAGE

OKAY THE WAY I AM

The LORD is for me; I will not be afraid.
What can a mere mortal do to me?
PSALM 118:6

Lord, sometimes I feel intimidated by other women, other moms, who seem to have their lives all together. They do five times as many activities with their kids, their cars are new and clean, their homes always seem to be immaculate—help me! Help me to be okay with who I am and the way You made me. Help me not to be afraid to invite them over for fear they will judge me. Help me to walk in the freedom of knowing You are for me and You love me just the way I am.
In Christ I pray.
AMEN.

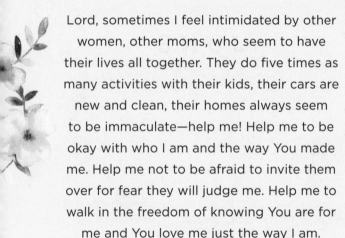

NOT A VICTIM

*Then [Goliath] said, "I defy the ranks of
Israel today. Send me a man so we can fight
each other!" When Saul and all Israel heard
these words from the Philistine, they lost
their courage and were terrified.*

I SAMUEL 17:10–11

Lord, just as Saul and the Israelites faced a
bully in their day, my children will face their
own today. Whether another student at
school or kid at the pool, they're out there
and I don't want any child to be a victim
of such horrible behavior. I can't always be
present to protect them, but You can.
So I ask You to please watch over them and
cover them with Your armor. Help me to
encourage them to be courageous and to
stand firm in the power they have through
Your Holy Spirit. Thank You, Lord.

AMEN.

DON'T LISTEN TO LIES

We demolish arguments...and we take captive every thought to make it obedient to Christ.

II CORINTHIANS 10:5 NIV

Thank You, Lord, for Your presence and the strength and courage it gives me for standing up to lies that play in my mind. Lies that say I'm not a good mom; lies that whisper I'm not very talented or I don't have much to offer; lies that get me to focus on what I don't have rather than what I do have. You are with me right now, and that's because You love me. Today I choose to walk in that love and the power it brings. Raise Your voice above the lies and hold me close throughout this day.
In Jesus' name.

AMEN.

DO HIS COMMANDS

Above all, be strong and very courageous
to observe carefully the whole instruction....
Do not turn from it to the right or the left, so
that you will have success wherever you go.
JOSHUA 1:7

Father, this verse reminds me once again
of just how important it is for me to not
only read Your Word but to do what it says.
In doing so, I am filled with Your strength
and courage to face any obstacle that
comes. Help me to teach this to my children
by my own example and also by holding
them accountable. I want them to have the
courage they'll need to do what is right
when they are tempted to do wrong.
In Your holy grace I pray.
AMEN.

THE POWER OF CORRECTION

Whoever spares the rod hates their children,
but the one who loves their children is
careful to discipline them.

PROVERBS 13:24 NIV

Lord, it is so difficult to discipline my child.
It's hard to see tears and a sad face, yet deep
down, I know it's important for lessons to be
learned and bad behaviors to be corrected.
Guide me in finding just the right way to correct
my child for their poor decisions. Please give
me the courage to remain firm in that correction
and not cover over the natural consequences,
so that they might learn big lessons from
small mistakes. It's hard, but when love is at
the core, I know it's very necessary.
Help me to remember this.
In Your mercy I pray.
AMEN.

COURAGE TO SHARE

The Jews of Corinth made a united attack on Paul and brought him to the place of judgment. "This man," they charged, "is persuading the people to worship God in ways contrary to the law."

ACTS 18:12-13 NIV

Jesus, I am inspired by Paul to have courage to share the gospel when opportunities arise. I want to be a bold witness for You, and for my children to be as well, but too often I stay silent. Help my love for You to be so strong, I can't help but share with others about Your saving grace. Whether it's my neighbor, a coworker, or someone at the checkout counter, I want to be a source of grace and truth that stands out from the rest of this world. In Jesus' name.

AMEN.

SIMPLY BELIEVE

*[Abraham] is our father in God's sight,
in whom [He] believed—the God
who gives life to the dead and calls
things into existence that do not exist.*

ROMANS 4:17

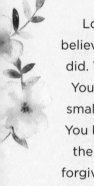

Lord, I want and need the courage to
believe—to simply believe the way Abraham
did. To believe that You are in control, that
You will provide, that You care about the
smallest of details I'm faced with. I believe
You have the answers to my questions and
the power to take my fear. I believe I am
forgiven and that Your grace covers me this
very moment. I believe You, and I thank You
from my heart for loving me.
In Your holy name.

AMEN.

IT'S OKAY NOT TO BE RIGHT

Don't resist an evildoer.
On the contrary, if anyone slaps you on
your right cheek, turn the other to him also.

MATTHEW 5:39

Father, when someone offends me, it's very
hard not to lash out. I want to spew a piece
of my mind and prove how much they are in
the wrong. But then that high road of Yours
convicts me otherwise, and, bottom line,
I want to please You more than I want to be
right. Give me the grace and the courage
not to seek revenge or justice on my own.
Help me to leave that up to You.
In Your name I pray.

AMEN.

JESUS, OUR HELPER

Our help is in the name of the LORD,
the Maker of heaven and earth.
PSALM 124:8

Lord, thank You for this reminder.
I get so focused on solving problems or
how I'm going to get more accomplished
and forget that You are my Helper.
You are but a whisper or plea away and You
are with me to help. I call out to You now,
Jesus. I want and need You to usher me
through all the demands on my plate today.
Help me to remember to call on You first.
I love You and thank You for loving me.
AMEN.

GOD IS STILL GOOD
WHEN HE SAYS NO

Even if [God] does not rescue us [from the
blazing fire], we want you as king to know
that we will not serve your gods or worship
the gold statue you set up.

DANIEL 3:17-18

Father, it's easy to praise and worship
You after You've answered a prayer with a
happy ending, but when You don't...when
the answer is no...I feel challenged to still
praise You. Increase my faith, fill me with
the courage and belief that You are still for
me, even when the answer is no. Help me to
grow even closer to You because of Your
no rather than to resent You for it.
I do love You so very much.

AMEN.

CHRIST SET US FREE

For freedom, Christ set us free.
Stand firm then and don't submit
again to a yoke of slavery.
GALATIANS 5:1

Lord, freedom always comes at a cost.
In the case of my salvation, freedom from
my sin came at the ultimate cost—Your life
in exchange for mine. In a world of scoffers
and haters, I am set apart for Your glory
and blessing. Help me never to look back,
but only look forward to serving You no
matter the pressure I face to conform to the
lies and darkness I see around me.
Help me teach my children to do the same.
I pray in the power of Your name.
AMEN.

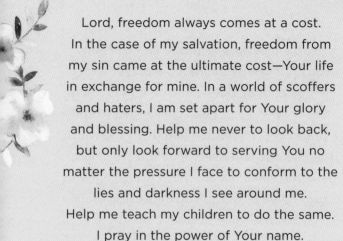

PRESS ON

*One thing I do: Forgetting what is behind
and straining toward what is ahead,
I press on toward the goal to win the prize
for which God has called me heavenward
in Christ Jesus.*
PHILIPPIANS 3:13-14 NIV

Lord, Paul's example of pressing on toward
the goal of God's call sounds so noble,
but here I am pressing on through the
dailiness of diapers, runny noses, forgotten
lunch boxes, and carpool lanes. Help me
to know and truly understand the glory in
motherhood. Help me have the courage
to resist the temptation to think my role
as a mom is anything less than one of the
highest callings You ever created.
Thank You, Lord.
AMEN.

THE GOOD IN CLOSED DOORS

Paul and his companions traveled...having been kept by the Holy Spirit from preaching the word in the province of Asia. When they came to the border of Mysia, they tried to enter Bithynia, but the Spirit of Jesus would not allow them to.

ACTS 16:6-7 NIV

Lord, when I think of the doors You've opened—
You have brought me such joy! Why, then,
do I get anxious and so easily call it quits when
You close others on my dreams? Help me, give me
the courage and faith I need to keep walking and
serving and pressing on until You clearly tell me
to stop. Help me not to give up. Help me to be of
good cheer and understand that sometimes I'm
just not ready to be where You want me to be and
that Your purpose is what matters most.

In Jesus' name.

AMEN.

WAIT FOR THE LORD

Wait for the LORD; be strong,
and let your heart be courageous.
Wait for the LORD.

PSALM 27:14

Father, it is hard to wait, especially while
living in such an "instant" world. Yet it's
an important virtue to have and to teach
young ones who are curious, anxious to
grow up, and who possess such adventure.
But living for You means doing things in
Your timing, not ours. Help me to teach this
not only as a command from Your Word,
but by my own example.
In Your strength and grace, I pray.

AMEN.

SPREAD HIS LOVE

You will have suffering in this world.
Be courageous!
I have conquered the world.
JOHN 16:33

Lord, I don't have to look far to see poverty, sickness, and oppression. It's even as close as my neighborhood and my child's school. No one is immune to suffering of some kind, including my family. I am so glad for the hope and the encouragement Your Word gives to press on and not give up. I could not imagine life without You, yet I see people all around who go through the motions in dire situations every day. Help me to spread Your love and be a vessel of grace to the hurting. In Your great name.
AMEN.

REACHING
OTHER MOMS

Love the Lord your God with all your hear,...
The second is, Love your neighbor as yourself.
There is no other command greater than these."

MARK 12:30-31

Lord, I meet other moms who don't know
You and it makes my heart feel heavy.
Give me courage to step out and invite
them over, let our kids play together, and
have fellowship in Your Spirit and presence.
Give me opportunities to invite them to
church to get a foretaste of what it's like
having You in their lives. I especially pray
that my children can have a godly influence
on their children. I want with all my heart
to reach these women with hope and
encouragement that lasts for eternity.
In Your sweet name I pray.

AMEN.

COURAGE TO ASK FORGIVENESS

*If...you remember that your brother or sister
has something against you, leave your gift
there in front of the altar. First go and be
reconciled...and then come and offer your gift.*

MATTHEW 5:23-24

Lord, I blown it before—I've lost my temper
and said things I should've never said in
front of my family. Help me never to do this
again—to make things right and hopefully
bring healing. Give me the courage I need
to simply ask for forgiveness with a sincere
heart, beginning now with You.
Please forgive me and help me to right
any wrong I've done. I love my family
and know You do too.
In Your grace and mercy I pray.

AMEN.

COURAGE
TO FORGIVE

If you forgive others their offenses,
your heavenly Father will forgive you as well.
MATTHEW 6:14

Father, I have been stewing and losing
sleep over an offense that someone did to
me, and I know there's no other solution
other than forgiveness. It's hard—
I honestly don't want to hold this in my
heart anymore. But I know letting go of it
is what's right and needed to bring healing.
Help me, give me the courage and faith
I need to truly believe that You see and
know all things, and that You will handle the
offensethis situation in Your own way.
In the meantime, You forgive,
now it is time for me to do the same.
In Your grace.
AMEN.

BE WHO HE WANTS YOU TO BE

Be satisfied with what you have, for He Himself has said, I will never leave you or abandon you. Therefore, we may boldly say, The Lord is my helper; I will not be afraid. What can man do to me?

HEBREWS 13:5-6

Father, I need courage to be the mom You made me to be and live the life You've called me to. Help me not to give in to the way the world tries to define moms. I want to raise my kids the way You lead me to and be okay with it. You know me and my children better than anyone. You know our needs and the ways You want to fill them. Help me be strong and confident in where You lead and how we'll get there.
In Your great name.

AMEN.

IT'S OKAY TO REST

The apostles gathered around Jesus and reported to Him all that they had done and taught. He said to them, "Come away by yourselves to a remote place and rest for a while."

MARK 6:30-31

Father, I get so tired from trying to keep pace with everything—work, school, after-school activities, the house, church... I want and need to rest, but then I feel guilty when I take time for me. Help me to break through the guilt of feeling inadequate because I struggle to keep up. Give me courage to turn off the lies that tell me I'm selfish and replace them with Your voice of truth. I want to rest and, deep down, I know it's what You want for me too.
In Your grace.
AMEN.

HONORING DADS

Love one another deeply as brothers and sisters. Outdo one another in showing honor.
ROMANS 12:10

Lord, being a mom is hard work, but it's also very hard for dads. The responsibility to help provide, not just financially, but spiritually, emotionally, physically, educationally—it's a lot. I pray for You to bless the father of my children with wisdom and the courage he needs to fulfill his role with abandon. Help me to help him be the best dad he can be to our children.
In Christ's name.
AMEN.

EQUIPPED FOR THE WORLD

Those who war against you will become
absolutely nothing. For I am the L<small>ORD</small> your
God, who holds your right hand, who says to
you, "Do not fear, I will help you."

ISAIAH 41:12–13

Lord, there is so much bad in this world for
my children to see. I want to shield them
from it all, yet they need to be equipped
for the realities they face every time they
leave our home. Give me the courage and
wisdom I need to do just that: provide Your
truths for knowing what is right and good.
Help me enable them to walk in the power
of Your presence and Your promises
to help and protect them.
And please help my heart be at peace.

AMEN.

VALUE IN MISTAKES

Though he falls, he will not be overwhelmed,
because the LORD supports him with His hand.

PSALM 37:24

Father, every time I see each of my children
about to make a mistake, I want to jump
in and keep it from happening. But I know
there is value in making mistakes and
learning from them. Give me the strength
and courage I need to keep quiet and
stay out of the way. I want them to learn
to lean on You more. I want them to trust
in Your help and how You can use every
circumstance for Your good—no matter
how big the mistake. But I need Your help—
it's very hard. In Your grace and mercy.

AMEN.

YOUR PLANS,
HIS PLANS

*I call to God Most High, to God who
fulfills His purpose for me.*

PSALM 57:2

Lord, as I watch my children's personalities
and talents blossom, it's hard not to plan
their lives the way I think they should go.
But I want Your plans for them to unfold—
they are so much greater than anything
I could imagine. Give me the courage to
let go of my preconceived ideas and look
intently at what You want for them.
Show me my purpose in steering them
toward where You want them to be.
You created them,
and I know You love them.
In Your great name.

AMEN.

STAND BESIDE, STAND IN FRONT

In Him we have boldness and confident access through faith in Him.

EPHESIANS 3:12

Lord, I'm not one for conflict, but there are times I need to stand in the gap for my children. There are bullies, teachers who openly teach against our faith, and negative forces in this world. Give me the strength I need for standing behind or beside them to enable and encourage. Give me courage for standing in front of them to guard or protect. Help me be an advocate when they aren't able to speak or act for themselves. By the power of Your Spirit in me, I want to claim the boldness that is mine as mother of my children.
In Your great name.

AMEN.

SHOWING YOUR FAULTS

*All have sinned and fall short
of the glory of God.*

ROMANS 3:23

Father, sometimes I try so hard not to make
mistakes in front of my kids—I don't want
them to see my faults on display. But that's
not being honest and true to them. Give me
courage not to be so on guard and, instead,
let them see me falter. Give me humility and
grace when I do so they can also learn not
to be ashamed of failing from time to time.
It's all part of being human and
understanding that no one is
perfect but You.
In Your grace and peace I pray.
AMEN.

FUN OVER FEAR

*Do not fear, for I am with you; do not be
afraid, for I am your God. I will strengthen
you; I will help you; I will hold on to you with
My righteous right hand.*

ISAIAH 41:10

Lord, the time is approaching!
My child is ready to learn to ride a bike.
And I get butterflies just thinking of falls,
scraped knees, and a bruised ego. I remember
how scary it was to learn to ride on two
wheels, and now I feel the same anxiety as I
step up to the teaching role. Please give me
courage so that confidence shines and the
experience will be more fun than fearful.
I so want this to be a good memory to
look back on for years to come.
I love You, Jesus.
AMEN.

TALKING THROUGH THE VALLEYS

You, Lord, are a compassionate and gracious God.

PSALM 86:15

Father, there are so many up and down emotions that a child's growing up brings. Heartbreak, sorrow, grief... Sometimes the drama can be too much and I just want to escape. I need Your help—it's not easy leaning into someone's struggle and not have all the answers. Give me courage to talk through the cares. Give me wisdom for when to speak and when to comfort. Give me compassion for walking through each valley to a renewed day of hope and healing. In Your comfort and love.

AMEN.

THE BEST ROLE MODEL

We will not hide them from their children,
but will tell a future generation the
praiseworthy acts of the LORD, His might,
and the wondrous works He has performed.

PSALM 78:4

Lord, it's pretty sobering to realize I am one
of the biggest influences in my child's life.
I want to be the best role model possible,
but sometimes I struggle and feel
insufficient. I need courage to face each
day—I'm so flawed. Help me hold on to
the promise that I am not alone on this
journey—You are with me to help, lead,
and guide. And Your grace is always
ready to cover where I fall short.
In Your great name.

AMEN.

LETTING GO

The Lord gazes down upon mankind from heaven where He lives. He has made their hearts and closely watches everything they do.

PSALM 33:13-15 TLB

Father, I want the courage it takes to completely release my children to You. Help me remember that each time we part ways, You are still with them and watching over them. Help me remember that You love them even more than I do, which is hard to grasp. Give me the courage to daily commit their lives into Your care as they discover and live out the purpose You created them for. I'm so grateful You've blessed me with being a mom and the joy that is mine by having them in my life.

In Jesus' name.

AMEN.

JULY

JOY

THE RADIANCE OF JOY

Those who look to Him are radiant with joy.

PSALM 34:5

Lord, this is true. I have seen people with a definite glow and presence because they love You. They radiate with joy— it is unmistakable and luring. It is a living testimony to the life You give and the hope You instill deep within the soul. Without You and the joy that You bring, life has no real meaning or purpose. Help me to realize the heavenly purpose that reigns here on earth and to walk by Your Spirit of joy in a way that not only my children but others, too, will take notice and want for themselves. In Your sweet name.

AMEN.

THE TRUE
SOURCE OF JOY

Then I will go to Your altar, O God;
You are the source of my happiness.

PSALM 43:4 GNT

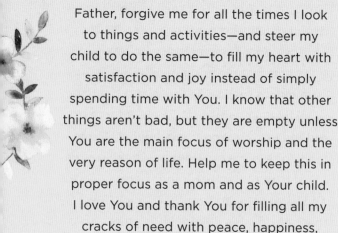

Father, forgive me for all the times I look
to things and activities—and steer my
child to do the same—to fill my heart with
satisfaction and joy instead of simply
spending time with You. I know that other
things aren't bad, but they are empty unless
You are the main focus of worship and the
very reason of life. Help me to keep this in
proper focus as a mom and as Your child.
I love You and thank You for filling all my
cracks of need with peace, happiness,
and Your faithful presence.
In Jesus' name.

AMEN.

TEST MY HEART

Deceit fills hearts that are plotting for evil;
joy fills hearts that are planning for good!

PROVERBS 12:20 TLB

Lord, test my heart and show me any way
that my actions—and the motives behind
them—are insincere or self-seeking.
Help me to be more deliberate in
showing love and kindness because,
when I do, I always feel Your peace laced
with a thread of joy within my heart.
And that is a great gift to carry throughout
the day as well as spread out onto others.
In Jesus' name and power I pray.

AMEN.

THE JOY OF
NEW BIRTH

Because of His great mercy He has given
us new birth into a living hope through the
resurrection of Jesus Christ from the dead.

I PETER 1:3

Jesus, I'll never forget the day I came to
know You as my personal Savior. I was
literally reborn into a new life with new
meaning. You gave me a new heart with a
new start. No, my problems didn't go away,
but I faced them with a new perspective
and a new resolve. You have brought me
joy I never thought I'd call my own, love I
never thought I'd have, and a life I never
dreamed could or would be possible.
Thank You for Your great love to me.

AMEN.

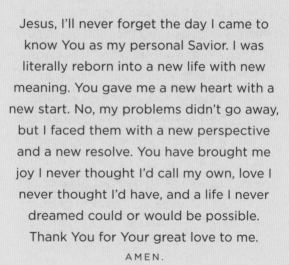

JOY IN HARD DAYS

On a good day, enjoy yourself; on a bad day, examine your conscience. God arranges for both kinds of days so that we won't take anything for granted.

ECCLESIASTES 7:14 THE MESSAGE

Lord, thank You for the days when joy leads the way and overshadows all of my problems. I consider them as customized gifts planned just for me. Help me hold on to joy during the hard days by remembering that a loving and caring God is in control. Help me to inspire my children to do the same, because they have hard days too. You are an anchor that holds us all steady and secure, and I am grateful.

All praise to You.

AMEN.

JOY ON THE SABBATH

This is a sacred day before our Lord.
Don't be dejected and sad, for the joy of
the LORD is your strength!
NEHEMIAH 8:10 NLT

Father, the Sabbath—Your holy day—
is the best reason for looking away from
hardships and devoting attention wholly
unto You. Yes, it's an act of obedience,
but it's also a gift of rest and rejuvenation
for the soul. You have blessed my life in so
many ways, my heart is strengthened when
I recount the abundance You have poured
onto me—in spite of the trials I'm in.
Help me to steer my family toward a day
of rest and focusing on You too.
We all benefit with renewed strength when
we honor Your holy day.
In Jesus' name.
AMEN.

JOY IN FORGIVENESS

How joyful is the one whose transgression
is forgiven, whose sin is covered!

PSALM 32:1

O Lord, I am humbled and thankful that
You are forgiving and gracious toward
me. The weight of my sin was heavy and
exhausting on my soul before I knew You,
but You cover me now with freedom and
new life. The burden I once felt has been
lifted and my guilt is gone. My heart is filled
with joy and praise for Your goodness and
for knowing I have a new, clean start today.
With thanksgiving and praise.

AMEN.

HE IS RISEN!

So [Mary Magdalene and Mary] left the
tomb quickly with fear and great joy, and
ran to tell [the good news to] the disciples.
MATTHEW 28:8 AMP

Jesus, what a rush of emotion and joy the
Marys must have felt when they found You
gone from the tomb! To see firsthand that
You had risen! It is the greatest miracle to
behold. Help me to share this phenomenon
with my children and what it means for
them—for us all. Thank You for Your
sacrifice and faithfulness and for Your Spirit
that now lives in us. Because You rose,
we all can live together for eternity!
All praise and glory to You.
AMEN.

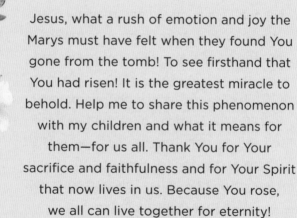

NEW SONGS OF JOY

*Sing a new song to Him; play skillfully on
the strings, with a joyful shout.*

PSALM 33:3

Lord, when I read this verse about singing
a new song to You, my heart smiles at the
thought of my children singing about You.
They are so sweet and pure. I join with them
and lift a song of praise to You—a simple
yet heartfelt hallelujah from me to You.
I have so much to shout about—Your love,
Your grace, Your mercy and forgiveness.
It's because of You I can sing songs of
praise and gladness and joy for Your
greatness and care. Thank You for
being so very good to me.
In Jesus' name.
AMEN.

JOY IN OPPOSITION

He brings the clouds to punish people,
or to water His earth and show His love.
JOB 37:13 NIV

Lord, I love that I can have joy no
matter how challenging my day may be.
When I face opposition or someone who is
offensive or the kids are being difficult,
I can shake off the residue and let joy fill my
heart anyway. I want to remain lifted by the
clouds of gladness You well up in my heart
today. And I pray it spreads onto others so
they will choose to delight in You too,
no matter what they are facing.
In the power of Your love.
AMEN.

JOY IN REPENTANCE

*There will be more joy in heaven over one
sinner who repents than over ninety-nine
righteous people who don't need repentance.*

LUKE 15:7

Father, it's a wonderful feeling to know
You are present, attentively listening and
waiting to heal every humble heart that
pours out words of confession and love
toward You. I rejoice with You in heaven
because it's literally a life-saving
experience. You give life and save life,
and that is the most precious celebration
of all. Thank You for not leaving us to
ourselves, but for saving us for You.
With songs of praise to You.

AMEN.

KINGDOM JOY

The kingdom of God is not eating and drinking, but righteousness, peace, and joy.
ROMANS 14:17

Father, this is so true—what the world says will bring satisfaction and happiness is the opposite of what You say. No amount of money, popularity, or fun living comes even close to the lasting, deep contentment that comes from abiding in You. Be with me today—be with my family—and help us all to be more content right where we are. I want my children to learn this truth sooner rather than later in life, so help me to be the example that points them to You.
In Jesus' name.
AMEN.

FRUITFUL JOY

The fruit of the Spirit is...joy.

GALATIANS 5:22

Lord, I can tell when I'm walking closely
with You because those are the times I
feel the most secure and joyful in my heart.
Help me to stay close and not get
distracted by things or people who pull
me away from You. I want Your spirit in me
to grow and reflect Your presence to my
family around me so there is no mistaking
that I am Your child and You are my great
and almighty Father.
Praise to You, from whom all blessings flow.
AMEN.

JOY FOR OUR FINAL DESTINATION

*[Jesus] was willing to die a shameful death
on the cross because of the joy He knew
would be His afterwards.*

HEBREWS 12:2 TLB

Jesus, it breaks my heart whenever I think
of the horrible and gruesome death You
endured on my behalf. There is no way for
me to repay You, yet You were still willing
to go to that cross. And because You did,
I rejoice from the depths of my heart that
I am spending eternity with You.
Thank You! Thank You for Your sacrifice
and the gladness I am able to
experience because of it.
In Your sweet name I pray.

AMEN.

THE JOY OF THE LORD

His lord said to him, "Well done, good and faithful servant; you were faithful over a few things, I will make you ruler over many things. Enter into the joy of your lord."

MATTHEW 25:21 NKJV

Father, because of You, I am doing things I never thought possible. The direction of my life, service on Your behalf, love extended to my family, my neighbors, the lost... Whatever I do, I want to hear the words "Well done, good and faithful servant." The joy that is mine as I grow in faith and responsibility is fulfilling beyond measure. Thank You for Your faithfulness and blessings. In Jesus' name.

AMEN.

BRING JOY
TO OTHERS

A joyful heart makes a face cheerful,
but a sad heart produces a broken spirit.

PROVERBS 15:13

Father, when I see any of my children with
a downcast expression, my heart feels
heavy with compassion. In spite of my busy
schedule and heavy load, help me to be
a source of comfort and a ray of love and
sunshine. Help me to permeate the blessing
of Your presence so they know they are
loved not only by me but by You as well.
Because of You, I'm able to have joy even
on the hard days, and I want that
same blessing for them.
With thanksgiving and praise.

AMEN.

JOY FOR ALL

*[The churches in Macedonia] have
been tested by great troubles.
And they are very poor.
But they gave much because of
their great joy.*
II CORINTHIANS 8:2 ICB

Lord, Your presence in my life brings such
comfort and delight, especially in difficult
times. Your anchor of hope and gladness
of heart are far greater than any of my
problems. I can freely give to others in far
greater need than me, because I want them
to hold the promise of Your love and the
fullness of Your joy the way I do.
Whatever it takes for You to become real
to someone in need, I want to do it.
In Jesus' name.
AMEN.

JOY IN FELLOWSHIP

*Every day [the believers] devoted
themselves to meeting together in the
temple, and broke bread from house to
house. They ate their food with
joyful and sincere hearts.*

ACTS 2:46

Lord, fellowship with other moms is one
of the greatest joys I know. That's because
there's a time and chance to love on them,
and be loved in return. Your love brings
healing to my heart and new energy to my
spirit. Sharing the heart of Your presence is
so sweet and lasting. Yes, eating is always
nice, but fellowship is food for my
soul and what satisfies most.
With thanksgiving and praise.

AMEN.

JOY IN TRIALS

Consider it a great joy...whenever you experience various trials, because you know that the testing of your faith produces endurance.

JAMES 1:2-3

Father, it's hard to consider it a joy in hardships and trials, especially those I have as a mom. But because Your Word says to, I will. I trust You—to be in control, to redeem anything that's lost, and to grow me in ways You want so I can be more powerful and effective for Your kingdom, beginning in my home. Knowing You're with me to guide my steps and lead the way, I can rest in the joy You bring, no matter the circumstances.

In Jesus' name.

AMEN.

JOY INCREASING

*Walk worthy of the Lord...bearing fruit
in every good work and growing in the
knowledge of God, being strengthened with
all power, according to His glorious might.*
COLOSSIANS 1:10-11

Lord, growing in Your knowledge, increasing in
strength and power,
bringing pleasure to You—knowing these are the
fruit of my efforts while serving You can't help
but bring joy to my heart. You are a wellspring of
abundance and the source of all that is good. Yes,
it's a "one day at a time" effort as I try not to be
overwhelmed with life as a mother, but I want to
share in and be part of the inheritance of joy that
You give. I want my family to be part of
that inheritance too.
In Jesus' name.
AMEN.

JOY IN JUSTICE

How glad the nations will be, singing for joy because You are their King and will give true justice to their people!

PSALM 67:4 TLB

Father, I am so glad You are a God of justice. You see all dishonest acts— You know the heart of every person. It is hard not to lash out at someone who's done wrong to me or one of my children, but I take rest in knowing You have great plans for me. Help me to claim the joy that is mine and not to focus my time and effort on others who have hurt me. I lift my heart to You.

AMEN.

HOLD ON TO JOY

You received our message with joy from the Holy Spirit in spite of the trials and sorrows it brought you.

I THESSALONIANS 1:6 TLB

Father, I love how, no matter how heavy and thick my trial, I am able to remain secure in the joy that You give. This is the day You have made, and I choose to overcome what I don't like about it with Your promises— promises of hope, of love that will not end, and of the contentment that comes from joy through Your Spirit that lives in me. Thank You for holding on to me as I hold on to gladness in You.

AMEN.

GLORIOUS JOY

Though not seeing Him now,
you believe in Him, and you rejoice with
inexpressible and glorious joy.

I PETER 1:8

Father, I do believe, and I rejoice with a
full and grateful heart for Your Holy Spirit,
who is very much alive in me. I see evidence
of Your presence all around in the smallest
details of my very life. You surround me
with indescribable peace regardless of
what I am facing. I can't not lift my words
of praise to You and smile from within
knowing I am loved and cared for
by You, the Creator of the universe
and the heavens.
In Jesus' wonderful name.

AMEN.

JOY IN HIS PRESENCE

Now to Him who is able to protect you from
stumbling and to make you stand in the
presence of His glory, without blemish and
with great joy.

JUDE 24

Lord, to stand in Your glory is almost
inconceivable for me to grasp, yet it's
true—as Your child, Your presence is
manifest in me. This brings great joy to
my heart considering where I came from
before knowing You. Help me always to
remember that You are with me, sharing
Your goodness while guarding my
steps and protecting my way.
In Your great name I pray.

AMEN.

JOY FOR TODAY

When I am filled with cares,
Your comfort brings me joy.

PSALM 94:19

O Father, You know the cares and concerns
on my heart today—and I'm so glad I
can bring them to You. Please wrap Your
comfort around me and fill me with Your
power and strength. Turn my worries for
tomorrow into joy for today that cannot be
broken. I love You so deeply and pray
in Your name.

AMEN.

LOST JOY

Joy has left our hearts; our dancing has
turned to mourning.
The crown has fallen from our head.
Woe to us, for we have sinned.

LAMENTATIONS 5:15–16

Father, I humble myself before You and
search my thoughts for any offensive
way in me. Please show me anything I do
that displeases You or any way I live that
hurts my testimony of Your gospel. I ask for
Your mercy and forgiveness, cleansing and
healing so that nothing will stop Your peace
and delight from dwelling in my heart.
I love You and pray this in Jesus' name.

AMEN.

ROBED WITH JOY

*The wilderness pastures overflow, and the
hills are robed with joy. The pastures
are clothed with flocks and
the valleys covered with grain.*

PSALM 65:12–13

Father, I love to soak in the beauty of
Your creation. It enraptures my eyes with
the divine touch of Your handiwork.
The abundant wildlife that roams, the
bright and colorful backdrops—it is all-
encompassing of how artistic and lovely
You are. No matter how busy my day gets,
I want to be in the pleasure of Your
company. A moment here, a few minutes
there...don't let me miss the splendor that is
mine when I take the time to enjoy You.
All praise be to You for such goodness.

AMEN.

JOY FROM HIS WORD

Your decrees are my heritage forever;
they are the joy of my heart.
PSALM 119:111 NRSV

Lord, I love Your Word—it is powerful
and alive. The promises, the advice,
the guidance—show me how to raise a
child and maintain my own personhood
as I grow in You. But even more, I get
to enter into Your world and learn more
about You—my Savior and my Redeemer.
And I love that it won't change—it stands
true day after day for my lifetime and my
child's lifetime. I know I can depend on the
consistency and permanence of Your ways,
and that brings comfort to my heart.
Thank You for such a gift.
In Jesus' name.
AMEN.

SECURE IN HIS JOY

[The Lord] will spread His wings over
you and keep you secure. His faithfulness
is like a shield or a city wall.

PSALM 91:4 CEV

Lord, I fully realize that You have my
family protected. None of us are in control,
I see that full well. And I take joy in knowing
that Your faithful love is our protection.
I pray that You will shield our home and fill
it with Your presence. Help all who enter
know that You are near. Help us all
to delight in this day and walk freely in
the safety and care that You give.
In Your name I pray, Jesus.

AMEN.

JOY FOR THE DOWNCAST

Let the bones you have crushed rejoice.

PSALM 51:8

Father, I pray for people I know who don't
have joy—whose spirits are crushed from
the weight of this world. Help me to be a
messenger of gladness in You to erase the
sadness that wants to overtake them. Help me
to show them there is hope and more to live
for than the shallow and false promises that
constantly disappoint. Give me courage to be
a light of Your joy to spread seeds of love that
bring healing and comfort that is real and true.
All praise to You.

AMEN.

THE JOY OF JESUS

*Now I [Jesus] am coming to You [Father],
and I speak these things in the world so
that [the disciples] may have My joy
completed in them.*

JOHN 17:13

Jesus, I am humbled that You prayed
to the Father for us to have Your joy.
This tells me I don't have to create joy for
myself—Yours is there for the taking and
choosing. On days that tear us apart,
we can pick ourselves up and embrace Your
joy. I think this is why You want our outlook
on life to be that of children—because they
live in the wonder of Your love. Help me
remember this with each smile and giggle
and outburst of laughter I hear in my home.
Thank You, Lord, for Your joy.

AMEN.

AUGUST

REST

REST FROM DEMANDS

*[Jesus] said to [the disciples], "Come away
by yourselves to a remote place and rest
for a while." For many people were
coming and going, and they did
not even have time to eat.*

MARK 6:31

O Lord, I know You understand the pressure
I feel with all the demands that are placed
on me each day—and there are a lot.
The list seems endless and my strength
and willpower get so strained. Please show
me the unnecessary burdens I'm putting
on myself, and give me Your strength to
complete the tasks that are truly important
for today. In Your Spirit I pray.

AMEN.

REST
IN TRUST

Trust in the Lord with all your heart,
and do not rely on your own understanding;
in all your ways know Him,
and He will make your paths straight.

PROVERBS 3:5-6

Lord, I take in a deep breath now and
exhale all of me that I can. I want to be
filled by more of You and less of me.
Help me to rest in the knowledge that You
are with me and involved in every detail of
my life story. I want to trust You with every
fiber of my being. Help me to let go of me
and my agenda and trust in Your love
and perfect way for this day.
In Your sweet name.

AMEN.

REST FROM THE CHAOS

God is not a God of disorder but of peace.

I CORINTHIANS 14:33

O God, life can be so chaotic, especially with all the kids' schedules and needs. It's hard to watch the news without feeling overwhelmed, and it's hard to live without feeling as though I'm always behind. Please come into this day with Your peace and calm. Bring order to my thoughts and control to my emotions. Surround me with the serenity of Your presence, and let it be bigger and stronger than all the distractions that vie for my energy. Help me rest by staying in stride with Your Spirit on the path You have set before me.

Oh, how I love You.

AMEN.

REST IN
HIS LOVE

Because the king trusts in the Lord,
he will never stumble, never fall;
for he depends upon the steadfast love of
the God who is above all gods.

PSALM 21:7 TLB

Father, I can't imagine living without Your
constant love. It's true, it's pure, it's healing,
and it's always here for me, no matter what.
Your love holds me up when I can't take
another step. It surrounds and protects me
from temptation and harm. I need it for my
very life. I want to rest in Your steadfast
love today as if it's the most important
thing in my world, because it is.
In Your holiness I pray.

AMEN.

REST FROM WORRIES

Don't worry about your life,
what you will eat or what you will drink....
But seek first the kingdom of God and
His righteousness, and all these things will
be provided for you.

MATTHEW 6:25, 33

Lord, I know that when I worry, it's because my focus is on my troubles and not on Your greatness. Help me to see Your face today and rest in complete faith that You are already filling my needs and working to solve my problems. I want simply to take You at Your word when You say not to worry and to believe with all my heart that You will provide at just the right time. In Your great name.

AMEN.

REST IN HIS CARE

Humble yourselves... under the mighty hand of God, so that He may exalt you at the proper time, casting all your cares on Him, because He cares about you.

I PETER 5:6-7

Father, I'm so glad You aren't a far-off God but are intimate and close and aware of all that weighs on my heart. I want to curl up in Your mighty right hand, let out a deep sigh, and close my eyes in complete trust in Your care. Help me carry this thought throughout my day and remember that You are in control and that You have the very best in store for me and my family.

I trust in You.

AMEN.

REST ON THE SABBATH

*The LORD blessed the Sabbath day
and declared it holy.*

EXODUS 20:11

Father, it's so easy to keep busy every day
of the week—it's no wonder I am so often
tired. Help me to set apart and guard one
day, Your day, for resting my body and
mind, and for worshiping You for Your
goodness. I know I am better for it,
and You are pleased when I do.
Thank You for rest, true and holy rest.
All praise be to You.

AMEN.

REST FROM
FAST-PACED LIVING

*Our God says, "Calm down,
and learn that I am God!"*
PSALM 46:10 CEV

Lord, life is always so fast. Every day flies,
and I'm often unsure what all the activity
is even for. And, I'm so sorry to say, I miss
You in so much of each day because I
constantly hurry from one thing to the
next. Please help me slow down. Help me
prioritize what's truly important and let the
rest go. I want to breathe deeper and enjoy
my time walking and working completely in
sync with You, sharing each moment with
You. In Your love I pray.

AMEN.

REST IN HONEST WORK

Seek to lead a quiet life, to mind your own business, and to work with your own hands, as we commanded you, so that you may...not be dependent on anyone.

I THESSALONIANS 4:11–12

Father, sometimes the dailiness of work feels monotonous, and I wonder if I am really making a difference to anyone.
Help me remember that all that I do is for You.
Help me remember that I'm to work as though I am literally working for You.
When I do, I feel tremendous satisfaction knowing I have done my best, that I'm right where You want me to be, and that the results are in Your hands to do with what You will.
I lift my praise to You.

AMEN.

REST FROM TECHNOLOGY

They feared the LORD but also served their idols. Still today, their children and grandchildren continue doing as their fathers did.

II KINGS 17:41

Father, I spend so much time on my computer and phone, I'm afraid at times they have more control over me than I have over them. And sometimes I feel more connected with the world than I do with You. Help me to have better balance—help me turn off my devices and spend time praying and reading Your Word and enjoying Your presence more. Help me to keep in perspective that they are tools and nothing more. Help me to teach this to my children as well. You are the one true Source of peace and rest. All praise be to You.

AMEN.

REST IN GRACE

My grace is sufficient for you,
for My power is perfected in weakness.

II CORINTHIANS 12:9

O Father, thank You for the gift of Your grace. Forgive me for forgetting that I am to walk in it every day. Help me to remember that it's okay to be weak, because when I am, I'm more reliant on You than ever. Help me to stop beating myself up for mistakes I've made and instead hold on to the full measure of grace You have instilled in my life. I want to rest in knowing that I don't have to be perfect, just devoted. In Your great name I pray.

AMEN.

REST FROM INJUSTICE

[The LORD] is a shield for those who live with integrity so that He may guard the paths of justice.

PROVERBS 2:7-8

Father, all around I see so many injustices. Life here on earth truly isn't fair for all. Seeing wicked people prosper, innocent lives suffer, and the proud be praised— I confess it's taxing on my soul. I remember, though, that You are a just God. And You promise to balance the scales of injustice in Your time and in Your way. Help me to rest from my inner desire to take matters into my own hands, but instead focus on Your lead and trust that You're in control.

AMEN.

REST IN HIS GOODNESS

*[Jesus'] divine power has given us
everything required for life and godliness
through the knowledge of Him who called us
by His own glory and goodness.*

II PETER 1:3

Father, You are so very good—You provide
so abundantly for all that I need.
Whether it's wisdom, understanding,
strength, food, rest, grace, forgiveness,
or love, You give all so freely to overflowing.
I cannot thank You enough for blessing me
the way You do. Forgive me for any ounce
of worry I still hold on to in spite of all of
Your kindness. Today I will rest in Your care
and dwell on Your goodness to me.

AMEN.

REST IN KNOWING

I am the LORD. I have called you
for a righteous purpose,
and I will hold you by your hand.

ISAIAH 42:6

Father, I think on all the promises written
in Your Word, and I believe that You
will keep them. I have believed this for
some time, but now I want to step from
believing You will into a place of knowing
You have. You've already planned the
answers to the mountains I face. You even
hear my cries before I hear them myself.
The peace that washes over my soul for
knowing this is indescribable.
Help me to rest in that peace today.
All glory and praise to You.

AMEN.

REST IN CREATION

I will meditate about Your glory,
splendor, majesty, and miracles.

PSALM 145:5 TLB

Lord, I love the beauty of Your creation
and the oneness with You I feel when I'm
in it. The sound of water flowing, the smell
of pine and cedar, the quiet waves of wind
flowing through trees, the birds bursting
forth in song... Meditating on it releases me
to breathe deeper and exhale all the stress
from my body. Thank You for the blessing
of the outdoors—it reveals a lovely and
pleasing part of Your nature for all to enjoy.
In the beauty of Your presence I pray.

AMEN.

REST FROM
THE NOISE

*[Jesus] withdrew from there in a boat to a
secluded place by Himself.*

MATTHEW 14:13 NASB

Jesus, there were times You withdrew from
the crowds and the noise to be alone with
the Father, and I want the same for myself.
There is noise all around, from the kids, TV,
radio, construction, vehicles—the clamor
is everywhere, and I need to unplug and
just be quiet. Help me to make time to
withdraw, to disconnect, and to immerse
myself in the peaceful rest that You give
without feeling guilty for doing so.
I only want to hear Your voice and feel
the soothing balm that it is for my spirit.
I humbly ask this in Your name.

AMEN.

REST IN QUIET

*[The LORD] lets me lie down in green
pastures; He leads me beside quiet waters.*

PSALM 23:2

Father, will You lead me to quiet waters
today? Even in the midst of my demanding
pace of life and clamoring noise all round,
will You lead me to the quietness of Your
heart? I want to feel every beat and hear
each whisper You put into my mind.
Slow my steps and guide my way so I'm in
perfect step with Your will. Help me rest
in Your presence and perfect peace.
In You I am whole and renewed.

AMEN.

REST FROM SORROW

My soul is weary with sorrow;
strengthen me according to Your word.
PSALM 119:28 NIV

Father, I need Your joy in a world that
is hard and heavy. There is so much
devastation, and I don't see signs of things
getting any better. Please give me Your
strength and power to resist the temptation
to get discouraged and depressed.
Fill me with courage and hope that I can
share with others who are struggling in life.
Help me to rest and remember that You are
carrying me, so I don't have to carry life's
burdens on my own. Thank You for Your
loving, outstretched arm toward me this
day.
AMEN.

REST IN FORGIVENESS

*There is forgiveness of sins
for all who repent.*

LUKE 24:47 NLT

Father, I'm so very grateful for the
forgiveness I have as Your child. To know
that sin won't be held against me is a
glorious relief. The weight of guilt that's
lifted, the joy I'm able to have, the closeness
I'm able to experience with You—all
because I'm forgiven. Please examine my
heart now and see if there is any offensive
way in me. Convict me of change I need to
make for my benefit as well as my family's,
and bless me with the continual cleansing
Jesus brings. In Your sweet name I pray.

AMEN.

REST FROM STRIVING

*What do people get for all the toil
and anxious striving with which
they labor under the sun?*

ECCLESIASTES 2:22 NIV

Lord, I really need Your help to stop striving. I know that when I do— and that is often—it's because I want something in my own timing and in my own way. I bring urgency to situations that aren't urgent, and I try to force events and people out of the natural state that You've preordained. I trust in You. I want Your way and lead for this day. Therefore, I will wait and act when You say it's time. In the meantime, I'm thankful to rest from striving. With thanksgiving I pray.

AMEN.

REST IN HIS REDEMPTION

Into Your hand I entrust my spirit;
You have redeemed me, LORD, God of truth.

PSALM 31:5

Father, thank You for redeeming me and
all the mistakes and wandering of my past.
You have breathed new life into what was
once dead; You have worked Your good
into the wrongs I've done; You've brought
healing to places of my heart that were
broken; and You've removed the guilt and
shame I used to carry. You've restored what
I thought was ruined. I put my hope and
trust in You now and for eternity.
Only You are worthy.

AMEN.

REST FROM THE NEED TO PERFORM

Even when we were God's enemies,
He made peace with us,
because His Son died for us.
ROMANS 5:10 CEV

Lord, I read Your Word and know that You love me just the way I am, yet I struggle with feeling as though I've got to do more, be more, and accomplish more in order to love myself, let alone receive Your love. Help me to truly grasp that Your love is not conditional—You want me and love me as I am. Help me turn off the lies in my mind that say otherwise, and help me to embrace the me You made, just as I am.

AMEN.

REST IN HOPE

Rest in God alone, my soul,
for my hope comes from Him.

PSALM 62:5

Father, there are so many things that vie
for what and where I place my hope.
And I confess that some are very appealing
and tempting. But I've learned that there is
only One true source from which real hope
comes, and that is You. So I rest in You
today—not another person or a full bank
account or a drama-free household, but in
You. No matter what. My eyes and heart are
on You. In Jesus' name.

AMEN.

REST IN HIS VICTORY

All the ends of the earth
have seen our God's victory.

PSALM 98:3

Father, thank You for the soul-filled rest that
is mine because of Jesus. He has overcome
the world. He has brought victory over
death for all of humanity—including me.
And now I can rest in knowing I am mighty
through His Spirit; I have escaped death
because of His scars; I can rest knowing I
have an eternal home. There may be battles
on this earth right now, but the final
war has already been won.
All praise be to Jesus.

AMEN.

REST IN
GOD'S WORD

LORD, Your word is forever;
it is firmly fixed in heaven.

PSALM 119:89

Father, I know I can always rest in the
promises in Your Word. It's the one Source
of truth that exists. Whenever I read
through the passages, You breathe life into
my very spirit and open my eyes to Your
faithfulness and love. It will stand forever in
time because You are eternal; it will never
change because You remain the same.
It's a precious gift to have access to You
and to have such sweet time together.
With thanksgiving in my heart.

AMEN.

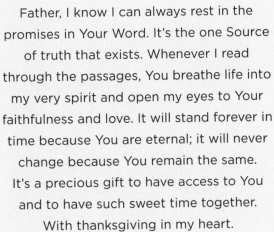

REST FROM A BROKEN HEART

The LORD is near the brokenhearted;
He saves those crushed in spirit.
PSALM 34:18

Lord, so many things today break my
heart—from relationships that have ended,
to the passing of loved ones, to the
anguish-inducing news headlines.
But instead of grieving another day,
I want to rejoice—in Your goodness and
mercy, in Your grace and love. I'm so
grateful for the renewal and hope You give.
Will You help me focus on all that is good
and life-giving today? Help me see the
sweet and simple blessings You offer and
rest in knowing You are with me.
Thank You, Jesus.
AMEN.

REST IN A
SURRENDERED LIFE

For me, to live is Christ and to die is gain.
PHILIPPIANS 1:21

Lord, I give my heart to You. Please take it
and mend its broken and bruised pieces.
Please smooth the jagged edges. I want my
life to be in Your hands. I surrender to Your
call. You are love, and I am in great need.
You are life, and I can't do mine on my own.
So please take me and grow me, mold me,
and use me—my life isn't life without Your
breath beating in my heart. I am Yours,
and I rest in the peace I have in You.
AMEN.

REST FROM ADVERSITY

David left Gath and took refuge
in the cave of Adullam.
I SAMUEL 22:1

Father, sometimes my problems feel so big,
I feel overtaken and overwhelmed. I need
Your help; I want to escape into Your arms.
Please carry me today and guard me from
the ocean wave that keeps wanting to beat
down on me. Keep me safe in the shadow
of Your wings, and guard me from the
enemy's attempts to discourage me.
I want to rest my weary soul in You.
Thank You for hearing my prayer.
AMEN.

REST IN GOD'S PROMISES

Through these He gave us the very great and precious promises. With these gifts you can share in God's nature, and the world will not ruin you with its evil desires.

II PETER 1:4 NCV

Lord, there are lies being told everywhere I go. And it is so hard to know who or what to trust and believe. This is why I am glad for Your Word—to discern what is false and to filter out the lies. I want to keep Your promises of love, wisdom, provision, and grace at the forefront of my mind. I sigh out the confusion and breathe in Your faithful words that keep me grounded and protected from believing untruths. By the power I have in Jesus' name I pray.

AMEN.

REST IN RECONCILIATION

At that moment the curtain of the temple was torn in two from top to bottom.
MATTHEW 27:51 NIV

Father, I'm so grateful to You for sending Jesus to this world. Because of His sacrifice and resurrection, we are no longer apart—I am reconciled to You, the Creator of the universe. There is no longer a veil separating You from humanity. We are together, and nothing can separate us from Your love. I am free to pray at any time of day or night. I have the hope of spending eternity with You, and Your Spirit is here to help me until that day. Thank You for sending Your Son and for the sacrifice He made. All glory and praise to You.
AMEN.

REST IN JESUS

Take up My yoke and learn from Me,
because I am lowly and humble in heart,
and you will find rest for your souls.

MATTHEW 11:29

Jesus, I want You and need You today.
You are the only One to bring pure and holy
peace into my difficult and often confusing
life. My gaze is on You. I take Your words to
heart because You are the best Friend I've
ever known. I love Your ways and want to
live them out for myself. I trust You with
my life because You are my very life.
You are all that is good, and I rest in You.
In Your great name I pray.

AMEN.

SEPTEMBER

FAITH

SURE ABOUT HIM

Then Jesus replied to her,
"Woman, your faith is great. Let it be
done for you as you want." And from that
moment her daughter was healed.

MATTHEW 15:28

Lord, I want the same faith this mother
had for her daughter's healing. Her belief
in Your power and willingness to heal was
unwavering. I want to be as sure about You
as she was. I want to know You and Your
ability without doubt or hesitation.
Please help my unbelief; help my faith to
increase while I decrease. Get my random
and distracting thoughts out of the way
so I can latch on to You with all my heart
and strength. You are so good.

AMEN.

NO ROOM
FOR DOUBT

*[Jesus] got up, rebuked the wind, and said
to the sea, "Silence! Be still!" The wind
ceased, and there was a great calm.
Then He said to [His disciples], "Why are
you afraid? Do you still have no faith?"*

MARK 4:39-40

Jesus, forgive me for doubting You—
for doubting Your ability and Your concern.
Even though storms rage in my life, I know
You are still with me; I just focus more on
the storm than on You. Increase my faith,
Lord. I want to believe You at face value
and know, without a doubt, that I do
not need to fear. You are in control.
You care. And I am holding onto You.
In Your sweet name I pray.

AMEN.

GUARD
YOUR HEART

Simon, Simon, look out. Satan has asked to
sift you like wheat. But I have prayed for you
that your faith may not fail.

LUKE 22:31-32

Lord, sometimes I feel like target practice.
And maybe I am because of my faith in
You—which is a threat to an enemy who
only wants to destroy. Please clothe me
with Your armor and guard my heart from
his attempts. No matter what my day holds,
no matter the challenge, I will praise You.
I will sing and shout my love and
devotion to a great and mighty God.
All glory and honor to You.

AMEN.

HIS PLANS ARE BETTER THAN MINE

"For I know the plans I have for you,"
declares the LORD, "plans to prosper you and
not to harm you, plans to
give you hope and a future."
JEREMIAH 29:11 NIV

Lord, I can't see what tomorrow holds,
not even what the end of this day holds,
but nothing is a surprise to You. Help me to
let go of my agenda and concerns and walk
in faith that You are with me and my family
and that You are for each one of us. I want
my faith to be evident and my joy made
complete because of the peace You give.
All my praise and worship to You.
AMEN.

CHOOSE FAITH

Let him ask in faith without doubting.
For the doubter is like the surging sea,
driven and tossed by the wind.

JAMES 1:6

Lord, this is so true. When I doubt You,
I become anxious and literally exhausted.
My problems become bigger than my belief
that You can and will provide in just the
ways our family needs. Please forgive me
and help me to choose faith. Help me to
take every thought captive to Your loving-
kindness to us in the past and hold onto
the belief that You will provide in the future.
You've promised. I love You, Lord.

AMEN.

HEAVENLY HANDIWORK

*By faith we understand that the universe
was created by the word of God,
so that what is seen was made from
things that are not visible.*

HEBREWS 11:3

Father, what an incredible beautiful
universe we live in! The planets,
constellations, galaxies, stars—the order in
which they exist, the mystery around them...
no man could have created such glory and
splendor. You and only You could have
created such an exquisite and magnificent
display for us to enjoy. Thank You for giving
us even a small glimpse of Your handiwork.
We are all blessed by it, and I give
You all the glory for it.
In Jesus' name.

AMEN.

SMALL FAITH, BIG RESULTS

For truly I tell you, if you have faith the size of a mustard seed, you will tell this mountain, "Move from here to there," and it will move. Nothing will be impossible for you.

MATTHEW 17:20

Lord, I'm so glad I only need faith the size of a mustard seed because sometimes that's all I can find within myself. Help me today not to worry about how much or little faith I have, but to be strong and confident in what faith I do have. Your power is so great, and it resides in me. And I feel assured in knowing that, with You, anything is possible.
Thank You for such a gift.

AMEN.

HOLD ON TO JESUS

*Let us hold on to the confession of
our hope without wavering,
since He who promised is faithful.*
HEBREWS 10:23

Father, I am holding on—I'm holding real
tight to the hope I have in You. How can
I not? Jesus has been so very faithful in
all ways imaginable. He has blessed me
with peace and filled me with unwavering
assurance of the salvation I have in Him.
You have promised never to leave. You have
promised a place in eternity with You.
You have promised that nothing can
separate me from Your love.
I hold on to You, dear Lord.
In Jesus' name.
AMEN.

WAIT FOR HIS WORD

I pray to GOD—my life a prayer—
and wait for what He'll say and do.
My life's on the line before God, my Lord.

PSALM 130:5-6 THE MESSAGE

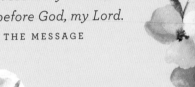

Lord, I am lost without Your love and
direction. I need answers to my questions
and understanding for my circumstances.
I pray and ask that You hear me now and
that I may never be so busy or preoccupied
to stop and listen for Your voice. I wait for
a Word from You that will stir my spirit
and assure me that You know I need.
I wait to see Your hand, Your touch in my
life, in my child's life, in our comings and
goings. My life is Yours—Your goodness
and grace is mine. And I love You.

AMEN.

FAITH PASSED DOWN

You were shown these things so that you
would know that the LORD is God;
there is no other besides Him.

DEUTERONOMY 4:35

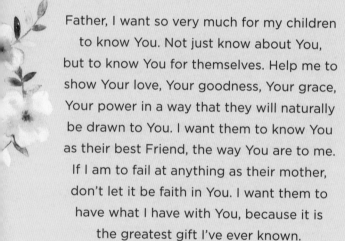

Father, I want so very much for my children
to know You. Not just know about You,
but to know You for themselves. Help me to
show Your love, Your goodness, Your grace,
Your power in a way that they will naturally
be drawn to You. I want them to know You
as their best Friend, the way You are to me.
If I am to fail at anything as their mother,
don't let it be faith in You. I want them to
have what I have with You, because it is
the greatest gift I've ever known.

AMEN.

STRONG FOR FUTURE GENERATIONS

You, LORD, will guard us; You will protect us from this generation forever.

PSALM 12:7

Father, it's so hard to bounce back after our hearts endured such pain, trauma, and destruction. I hate it when the enemy wins. It's during these times, though, that I'm reminded of the importance of remaining strong in faith, strong in the power we have in You, and strong for our children and future generations. You, Lord, are our protection and shield, and You have won the war for our souls. All glory and praise be to You.

AMEN.

FINDING KINDRED SPIRITS

Let us watch out for one another to provoke love and good works, not neglecting to gather together, as some are in the habit of doing, but encouraging each other.
HEBREWS 10:24-25

Lord, I know I'm not meant to live out my faith on my own—You created us for relationships. Will You please give me wisdom for finding a few other mom friends who love You and are committed to You? My heart feels bruised from past experiences. I need fellowship with other women in a way that is safe and nonjudgmental, encouraging and uplifting. Help me to be the same kind of friend in return. In Your name I pray.
AMEN.

A HEART
OF RESPECT

*Wives, submit yourselves to your own
husbands so that, even if some disobey
the word, they may be won over without a
word by the way their wives live when they
observe your pure, reverent lives.*

I PETER 3:1-2

Father, please soften my heart.
Help me to have understanding and patience
with the father of my children. He is not
perfect, but he tries. Help me to treat him with
the respect he deserves even when I don't feel
like it. I want to be an example to our children
so they will grow in faith that is honoring to
one another and to You. But some days it's
hard. Help me to draw from Your strength and
remember that I am not perfect either.
In Your grace and mercy I pray.

AMEN.

HE KNOWS
YOUR NEEDS

*You can be sure that God will take care
of everything you need, His generosity
exceeding even yours in the glory
that pours from Jesus.*
PHILIPPIANS 4:19 THE MESSAGE

Lord, some days I fear of failing my family.
There are so many needs, and I try to meet
them, but I feel like I fall so short at times.
I think this fear is Your way of showing me
that I am not meant to carry everyone's
burden. That is what You are for, and I often
forget. Help me to do what I can and trust
that You have all of us covered—
You know our needs even before we do.
Help me to rest in that today.
Thank You, Jesus.
AMEN.

REMEMBER WHAT HE HAS DONE

*I recall all You have done, O Lord....
[Your wonderful deeds] are constantly in my
thoughts. I cannot stop thinking about
Your mighty works.*
PSALM 77:11-12 NLT

Father, when I think about my trials, my
children's struggles, our family's challenges,
it's hard not to lose ground in my faith.
Help me redirect my focus on what You
have done in the past. Your faithfulness and
loving-kindness, Your answers to prayer,
Your blessings I didn't even ask for—they
are too numerous to count. Thank You for
Your provision in the past, and for how You
will help us today and in the future.
In Your great and mighty love, I pray.
AMEN.

HIS PLANS
ARE PERFECT

Many are the plans in a person's heart,
but it is the LORD's purpose that prevails.
PROVERBS 19:21 NIV

Lord, when I read these words,
I am reminded that I am not in control,
although sometimes I forget. You are at the
helm of my life. I can plan and prepare all
I want to, but it is Your will that wins.
And thank goodness for that—I wouldn't
want it any other way. I rest in knowing I
don't have to be in control—it's not my job.
My faith lies in knowing You are.
May Your will be done today.
In Jesus' name.
AMEN.

GOOD FOOD
FOR THOUGHT

Whatever is true, whatever is honorable...
whatever is pure, whatever is lovely,
whatever is commendable—if there is any
moral excellence...dwell on these things.

PHILIPPIANS 4:8

Father, I know that what I let my children watch
on TV or listen to on their playlist or play on their
computer games affects their minds. And I want
their minds to be fed with what is pure and good
and uplifting and true. The same is true for me—
I must guard what I allow in my world or my
faith is compromised. The blog posts I follow, the
music I play, the movies and shows I watch... Lord,
help me to be as mindful of what I see and hear
as I am for my family. Help me to set the bar for
strengthening faith in our home.
In Jesus' name.

AMEN.

OUR FAITH, HIS FAITHFULNESS

These [trials] have come so that the
proven genuineness of your faith...
may result in praise, glory and honor.
I PETER 1:7 NIV

Lord, when I look back on trials I've
endured, I see how my faith has grown.
I see Your faithfulness to me, and I see how
Your grace has shielded me. I must believe
the same will be true now and in the future.
I know You are with me to help and to
uphold with strength and care in just the
ways I need. Thank You for the hope You
give and the love You pour into my life.
Thank You, Jesus.
AMEN.

ALL IN

*Those who belong to Christ Jesus have
crucified the flesh with its passions and
desires. If we live by the Spirit, let us also
keep in step with the Spirit.*

GALATIANS 5:24-25

Father, I want to be more than just saved by
Your grace—I want my life to be all in with
You. I want to walk by Your Spirit and have
the faith I need to stay there. When I can't
see over the next hill, help me to remain
firm in my trust, because You can see over
and beyond. Help me not get ahead in
anticipation or behind in apathy.
I want to walk in step with my
gracious and loving Savior.
All praise be to You.

AMEN.

HIS TIMETABLE

*Wait for the L*ORD*; be strong, and let*
your heart be courageous.
*Wait for the L*ORD*.*
PSALM 27:14

Lord, it's hard to wait. I want to make things
happen faster than they are, but I can't.
I'm just not able. But I can stop and look to
You for strength and assurance, so that's
what I'm doing now. Even if I must repeat
it throughout this day, I will hold on to my
faith in You, that You are working this very
minute to answer prayer, to show Your
presence, and to remain in control.
All glory to You.
AMEN.

FAITH FOR TODAY

When I am afraid, I will trust in You.
In God, whose word I praise, in God I trust;
I will not be afraid.

PSALM 56:3-4

Father, sometimes my faith, my patience,
my belief gets tested to the brink.
I don't understand some of the trials You
allow, but I guess I don't need to. I only
need to keep my eyes on You and trust that
You are working all things for my and my
family's good. Help me not to think about
tomorrow, but to be in the present,
because this is where You are—with me
now. You've been faithful in the past, You
will be faithful today and the days to come.

AMEN.

PRAYING FOR OTHERS

Peter was kept in prison, but the church
was praying fervently to God for him.
ACTS 12:5

Father, thank You for prayer and the faith
that it gives. I can tell when someone is
praying for me—I have a supernatural
lightness to my spirit, and You feel very
close. I feel encouraged in my faith, and it's
a wonderful feeling. Help me remember to
take time to pray for others so they have
the same blessing for getting through their
day and circumstances. I especially pray for
my family—each heart and mind—as they
go through their day. May we all walk in
strength and confidence that comes with
knowing You. In Jesus' name.
AMEN.

HE IS OVER ALL

Abraham believed God, and it
was credited to him as righteousness,
and he was called God's friend.

JAMES 2:23

Lord, can I face the realities of my life and
simply believe You are in them? It should be
easy to believe You reign and that You're
in control. Your faithfulness has proved
itself over and over again. Why, then, do I
hesitate to trust You with my whole heart?
Why do I constantly try and take over as
though I know best? Lord, I want more
faith, so I take pause today, step back from
my plans, and simply believe that You are
indeed over all. In faith I pray.

AMEN.

CHILDLIKE FAITH

*The LORD...hears the
prayer of the righteous.*
PROVERBS 15:29

Father, how I love to hear my children pray.
When they do, I am reminded of why You
love pure and innocent faith, because that's
what they have. Help me weed out all my
doubt and pray to You without hesitation,
void of disbelief, and free of worrying
whether or not I'm saying the right thing.
Give me a childlike faith that opens the
floodgates of prayer from my heart to
Yours, and simply believes. I love You,
Jesus, and I know You love me too.
AMEN.

DECIDE OUT OF FAITH, NOT FEAR

Don't worry about anything, but in everything, through prayer and petition with thanksgiving, present your requests to God.

PHILIPPIANS 4:6

Lord, I have so many decisions to make, and it's hard to know if I'm making the right ones. There are so many "what ifs" that get in the way of clear thinking and hearing Your voice. Please help me to be wise. Help me to make decisions out of my faith and belief in You, and not out of fear that competes for attention. In Your power I pray.

AMEN.

IN THE WORLD, IN HIM

The world offers only a craving...for everything we see, and pride in our achievements and possessions. These are not from the Father, but are from this world.
I JOHN 2:16 NLT

Father, being in this world and not of the world is just plain hard. And if it's hard for me, it's very hard for my child—it's hard for all children. There's a constant bombardment of things to buy and pressure to always be having fun. What happened to just being still? In the end, the only thing that satisfies is knowing You—no matter what we're doing. Help me create a healthy balance, with You tipping the scales. Beginning with me, help our home to be a place that points to the lasting fulfillment You bring.

AMEN.

NEVER ALONE

Let us run with endurance the race that lies before us, keeping our eyes on Jesus, the Source and Perfecter of our faith.

HEBREWS 12:1-2

Father, it's so hard and exhausting being a mom. I only have so much time, energy, and know-how for my children. Help me to endure. Help me to keep going and trusting and believing that You are with me, and that You will help. My faith in You keeps me going, so I need a lot of it. My eyes are on You as I draw from the strength and power that You give. In Jesus' name.

AMEN.

NO LONGER MY FAITH

When [Jesus] entered the house, the blind
men approached Him, and Jesus said to
them, "Do you believe that I can do this?"
They said to Him, "Yes, Lord."
MATTHEW 9:28

Lord, I want my children to have a strong
and sincere faith in You, but I can only do
so much. There comes a point and time
when they must have their own faith.
Unless I'm helping, get me out of the way.
My hope is that Your Spirit of love will
be far more attractive to them than any
tempting lure the enemy places in their
lives. In the power of Your name, I pray.
AMEN.

FAITH IN
HIM ALONE

Jesus replied to [the disciples],
"Have faith in God."

MARK 11:22

Lord, as much as I love You, I still struggle
to get "faith in You" right. I know this is
true because of how disappointed I get
whenever the answer I want to a prayer
doesn't come. My struggle is a tug of war
between faith in the way You answer a
prayer and faith in You, no matter what
the answer is. The same is true about
having faith in other people more than I
have faith in You. It's a constant circle of
disappointment. Help my eyes and faith
stay fixed on You, and nothing else.

All glory to You.

AMEN.

HE IS WATCHING

The LORD—His throne is in heaven.
His eyes watch;
His gaze examines everyone.
PSALM 11:4

Lord, I believe. I believe You are with me now, and You are with me always. I believe You are watching and that You see the things that bruise my heart and sap my strength. You see my struggles and know my joys. You "gaze" upon my life, and I am comforted. Thank You that I can call to You at any time and that Your love comes down in just the ways I need. I'm so grateful for Your unending love toward me.
In Your gracious name I pray.

AMEN.

OCTOBER

WISDOM

FEAR THE LORD

The fear of the LORD is the beginning
of wisdom; all who follow His
instructions have good insight.
PSALM 111:10

Father, I am still learning what this means—
to fear You. Not the kind of fear that comes
with guilt, but the kind that reverences Your
very name and the nature of Your power.
I do want to be wise in a world that is filled
with counterfeits and liars. You are the One
who is real and lasting. You are truth and
love, and I am so grateful that You love
me. Help me impart this fear, this love, this
worship and praise to my children as they
grow and seek truth for themselves.
In Your great name.
AMEN.

WISDOM
IN SEEKING

*The LORD looks down from heaven o
n the human race to see if there is one
who is wise, one who seeks God.*

PSALM 14:2

Lord, having a child brings so many new
unknowns to life. Am I a good mom?
Will I be able to provide for all the needs?
Will I be a good enough influence for
showing Your love? What will I do when I
don't have all the answers? Help me not to
focus so much on the questions but more
on You in the here and now. Help me to
trust You more and rest in knowing You are
always here to help, lead, and guide.
Give me wisdom for the circumstances
that each day brings, one day at a time.
In the power of Your name.

AMEN.

SEIZE THE MOMENT

Mary...sat at the Lord's feet listening to what
He said. But Martha was distracted by all
the preparations that had to be made.
LUKE 10:39-40 NIV

Father, sometimes I get so busy—too busy—
and I miss out on seizing moments with
my child to teach, to love, and sometimes
just to be together in silence. I need better
balance and the wisdom to know what that
looks like. There is always so much to do,
but how much of it is self-created and how
much is of You? Help me to be sensitive
to Your voice and Your leading so that the
most important moments are grasped
and held for making good memories.
In Your sweet presence I pray.
AMEN.

TEACHABLE MOMENTS

I will instruct you and show you the way to go; with My eye on you, I will give counsel.

PSALM 32:8

Father, I need wisdom for the teachable moments You provide. A failing grade, losing a game, getting cut from the team, not getting picked for the play—these are difficult and real situations to work through with the kids, and each personality requires its own response from me. Through all of these moments, I want to convey love—not only mine, but Yours as well. Help me direct each heart toward You to instill what You know they need to hear at just the right time. I trust in You.

AMEN.

WISDOM FOR
THE JOURNEY

Trust GOD from the bottom of your heart;
don't try to figure out everything on
your own. Listen for GOD's voice in
everything you do, everywhere you go;
He's the one who will keep you on track.

PROVERBS 3:5-6 THE MESSAGE

Lord, I see every day that You are working in
my life and in my family's life. But I get anxious
because I don't always understand what You
are doing or what Your plan is. Challenges
seem to come out of left field, and I can't
make sense of what You're trying to teach or
reveal or accomplish. Please give me wisdom
for navigating the twists and turns ahead. Help
me to trust You more and rest in the fact that
You are up to something for our good,
no matter what our circumstances may imply.

AMEN.

CORRECTING WITH CARE

*The one who loves their children
is careful to discipline them.*

PROVERBS 13:24 NIV

Lord, my child's rebellious behavior is
so stressing and frustrating. It seems that
nothing I've tried is working—the actions
are even getting worse! I need Your help!
I need Your wisdom for correcting the
behavior with care without breaking the
spirit. This must be only a foretaste of how
You've felt during times I've strayed.
All I can say is, I'm sorry—very sorry.
Please forgive me and help me now to
parent with any and all wisdom You will
give. I trust in You to know what's best.

AMEN.

GODLY CHOICES

Plans fail when there is no counsel,
but with many advisers they succeed.

PROVERBS 15:22

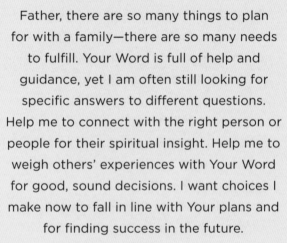

Father, there are so many things to plan
for with a family—there are so many needs
to fulfill. Your Word is full of help and
guidance, yet I am often still looking for
specific answers to different questions.
Help me to connect with the right person or
people for their spiritual insight. Help me to
weigh others' experiences with Your Word
for good, sound decisions. I want choices I
make now to fall in line with Your plans and
for finding success in the future.

AMEN.

DIFFERENT CHILDREN, DIFFERENT NEEDS

The LORD gives wisdom; from His mouth come knowledge and understanding.

PROVERBS 2:6

Father, my children are all so different—
their personalities bring excitement and fun to
our home, as well as varying challenges.
I want to inspire each heart to know You and
love You. I also need wisdom for teaching and
correcting in ways that speak best to their
individuality and uniqueness. What works for
one doesn't work as well for another.
I look to You and Your Word for how to be the
best mom I can be in all types of situations—
and there are a lot. I'm so glad to know
I am not alone in this journey.
I'm so glad I have You to help.

AMEN.

WISDOM
IN FINANCES

I know both how to make do with little,
and I know how to make do with a lot.
In any and all circumstances I have
learned the secret of being content.

PHILIPPIANS 4:12

Lord, I need wisdom in our finances.
How to budget better, how to let you guide
my giving, how to have the discipline to pay
off debt, and still reserve a little money for
enjoyment. Life can't be all work and no play.
Help me to find ways to make memories
that don't cost a lot, or even better, nothing
at all. Help us to enjoy the simple things
while just being together. There are so many
temptations to spend money we don't have.
Guide me in my choices. Thank you for the
resources You've provided.

AMEN.

WISDOM IN GIVING

Each one must give as he has decided in his heart, not reluctantly or under compulsion.

II CORINTHIANS 9:7 ESV

Father, there are so many needs in the world, and so many nonprofits that need money to operate. It's hard to know which ones to give to. And then when I think of one to support, there's the question of whether or not they are honest with how they use funds. Please give me guidance for where You'd like me to give—of money, of time, of items to donate. The needs are great, and I want to help, but I also want to be wise. Give me wisdom about my giving.

AMEN.

THE HEART OF THE MATTER

*There is one who speaks rashly,
like a piercing sword; but the tongue
of the wise brings healing.*

PROVERBS 12:18

Lord, please give me wisdom about how
to open up conversations that will get to
the root of the matter. I want to provide an
approachable and safe place where hearts
are free to share, and love can thrive.
Lord, help me foster a bond with my
children so they know they can tell
me anything, and I will love them
unconditionally. Help them to know that
I am in their corner, now and always.
Help me in this, Lord.

AMEN.

WISDOM FOR THE TRUTH

By examining [Paul] yourself you will be able to discern the truth about these charges we are bringing against him.

ACTS 24:6

Father, it hurts to see discouragement in my child's eyes. In those times, I need wisdom for how to probe and find out how I might make things better. I also need wisdom for when to speak up and when to step back and allow room for personal growth. I know this is training ground for learning ways to make peace or develop thicker skin and endure. This motherhood stuff can be so hard at times. Thank You for listening, Lord.

AMEN.

CLARITY IN CHOICES

*If any of you lacks wisdom, he should ask
God—who gives to all generously and
ungrudgingly—and it will be given to him.*
JAMES 1:5

Father, there are so many options and
opportunities these days for children
to grow, excel, and become amazing
human beings. There are so many, I feel
overwhelmed at times just thinking about it.
Please give Your wisdom for knowing which
ones to say yes to and which ones to say no
or not yet to. I'm grateful for having such
choices, but I also don't want extra activities
to distract from church and the activities
there that have a more obvious eternal
value. Please give me clarity for the choices
ahead. In Your grace and mercy I pray.

AMEN.

WISDOM IN OBEDIENCE

I hurried, not hesitating to
keep Your commands.

PSALM 119:60

Lord, You know what is best. Your timing is perfect. You care more about my character in obedience to You than in my outward lifestyle. Forgive me for the times I've hesitated to do what I believe You are leading me to do. I want to be ready— ready to move, to serve, to act, to carry out whatever ways You want to use my children and me in Your kingdom. Help me to hold my agenda loosely and be ready to go when Your voice speaks. I trust in You.

AMEN.

WHEN TO HOLD ON, WHEN TO LET GO

*A time for planting and a time
for uprooting what was planted.*
ECCLESIASTES 3:2 CEB

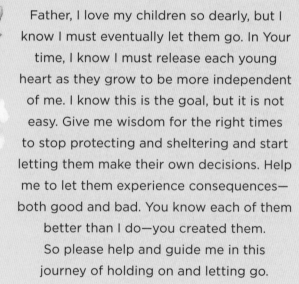

Father, I love my children so dearly, but I
know I must eventually let them go. In Your
time, I know I must release each young
heart as they grow to be more independent
of me. I know this is the goal, but it is not
easy. Give me wisdom for the right times
to stop protecting and sheltering and start
letting them make their own decisions. Help
me to let them experience consequences—
both good and bad. You know each of them
better than I do—you created them.
So please help and guide me in this
journey of holding on and letting go.
AMEN.

BE HUMBLE

Moses was a very humble man,
more so than anyone on the
face of the earth.

NUMBERS 12:3

Lord, if there's one thing You don't like it's pride. And one thing that's hard not to do is compare my child with other children. Please remove any judgment that tries to creep into my mind, and remind me that all children were created by You and loved by You. Don't let me compare my mothering skills with another mom's. Remind me that we all have our weaknesses and strengths—I am no better or worse. It's by Your grace I am able to fulfill my role as a mom at all.

I couldn't do it without You.

In Christ's name.

AMEN.

SELFLESS THINKING

Be kind and compassionate to one another, forgiving one another, just as God also forgave you in Christ.

EPHESIANS 4:32

Lord, spats among kids seem to be constant, and it's often hard to know how to handle them in a way that brings change in behavior and not resentment. Please give me wisdom for teaching reconciliation and restoration, forgiveness and selfless thinking. Help me to show kindness and, in turn, influence my children to be kindhearted and giving. Protect us with Your spirit of love and peace. Give us all a mindset of unity.

AMEN.

TOO MUCH WORLD, NOT ENOUGH GOD

He will keep in perfect peace all those who trust in Him, whose thoughts turn often to the Lord!

ISAIAH 26:3 TLB

Father, I confess that while I want Your wisdom and peace, I spend a lot of time focusing on my phone and computer, which connect me more to the world than to You. Help me to put them aside and make quiet time with You a high priority every day. Help me to discipline myself to go to bed a little earlier so I can get up a little earlier to begin each day concentrating on You and Your Word. Because when I do, I feel calmer and more sensitive to Your voice over all the other distractions that come. I love and worship You.

AMEN.

HE IS ALWAYS THERE

*The L*ORD *loves justice and will*
not abandon His faithful ones.
PSALM 37:28

Father, it's hard not having help with the
kids. But I believe Your Word that says
You are just and faithful. Please impart
Your wisdom for parenting and instilling
the truth that You are with us every day,
through every joy and every challenge.
I want my kids to know who their heavenly
Father is and how much You love them.
In Jesus' name I pray.
AMEN.

SLOW DOWN AND DECIDE

Listen and hear My voice.
Pay attention and hear what I say.
ISAIAH 28:23

Father, my schedule is so full, I sometimes
have to make split-second decisions in
order to get everything done. But that
makes me nervous—it can set me up for
more problems than not. Give me the
patience not to rush to a conclusion or
decision until I've heard from You. I want
to be wise in how I approach what I'll do,
where I'll go, and how I'll spend my time.
I want to be in the center of Your will.
I don't want to miss out on the blessings
You have in store when I follow Your lead
and timing. My heart and life are Yours.

AMEN.

WHAT IS MEANINGFUL, WHAT IS RIGHT

Jesus said, "No procrastination.... You can't put God's kingdom off till tomorrow. Seize the day."
LUKE 9:62 THE MESSAGE

Lord, with friends and family who are sick, struggling, and burdened with unexpected problems, I can't help but think of making every day count. I don't know what will happen to me or my child from one day to the next. Give me wisdom for doing what is most important for eternity—every day.

Let me not waste time on what doesn't matter in Your overall plan for our lives. I don't want any regrets, wishing I had spent more time doing other more meaningful things than what I am doing right now. Thank You for life and the abundance You bring.

AMEN.

LISTEN FOR
HIS VOICE

Guide me in Your truth and teach me,
for You are the God of my salvation;
I wait for You all day long.

PSALM 25:5

Father, sometimes my circumstances
leave me with so many questions about
how to respond to choices I'm faced with.
What do I do next and when do I do it?
What to say, what not to say. The easy route
is the most appealing, but it's not always the
one You want me to take. I need Your wisdom
to direct my thoughts for making good
decisions that complete Your plan and my
purpose. I want to hear Your voice clearly—
not to hear what I want to hear, but to hear
what You have to say. I simply need You.
Oh, how I love to praise You.

AMEN.

LIGHT ON
A DARK DAY

You are the light of the world.
A city situated on a hill cannot be hidden.
MATTHEW 5:14

Father, I need Your wisdom for navigating
through the dark spots of this world.
Help me to shine Your light in fresh, new
ways—ways that will make the darkness run
and hide. Help me to guide my children so
they remain lights of truth and hope. I pray
for You to protect our minds and hearts
from the outside elements that influence so
many people toward evil and away from
the power of Your saving grace.
In Jesus' name.
AMEN.

HIS GIFTS,
HIS GLORY

According to the grace given to us,
we have different gifts.

ROMANS 12:6

Father, as my children grow older
and mature emotionally and spiritually,
I see their gifts and talents blossoming.
Help me to help them develop their gifts
to the fullest degree. Help me discern what
activities and classes would most help
them experience the joy and satisfaction
that are theirs as they advance to full
measure. Mostly, give me wisdom for
how to inspire and encourage them for
using their gifts for Your glory.
In Jesus' name.

AMEN.

HOLDING ON, LETTING GO

*There is an occasion for everything, and a
time for every activity under heaven.*
ECCLESIASTES 3:1

Father, as I think about my children getting
older and the dating scene, preparing for
college, driving—I really need Your help and
wisdom for every curve in the road to come.
Help me know when to put on the brakes and
when to hand over the keys. Help me find
a healthy line between too much freedom
and not enough independence. I know that
none of this is new to You, but it's an uphill
climb I've not been on before, and I can't do
it alone. Thank You for the assurance of Your
presence and the reminder that You love
them as much or even more than I do.
In Christ's name.
AMEN.

HE KNOWS
WHAT'S BEST

All a person's ways seem right to him,
but the Lord weighs motives.

PROVERBS 16:2

Lord, I am certainly learning the truth in
this verse. Whenever faced with a problem,
I so often make decisions or plan to do
something out of fear or discontentment.
Fear that comes from dwelling on all the
"what ifs" and being discontent rather than
at peace with what I have. I am glad You
close doors and frustrate my efforts when
You know my motives are not healthy or
pleasing to You. I love Your wisdom over my
life, and I trust that You always know
what's best for me and my family.
In Your grace I pray.
AMEN.

MEDITATE ON GOD'S WORD

Righteous chews on wisdom like a dog on a bone.... His heart pumps God's Word like blood through his veins.

PSALM 37:31 THE MESSAGE

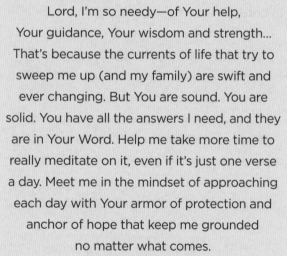

Lord, I'm so needy—of Your help,
Your guidance, Your wisdom and strength...
That's because the currents of life that try to
sweep me up (and my family) are swift and
ever changing. But You are sound. You are
solid. You have all the answers I need, and they
are in Your Word. Help me take more time to
really meditate on it, even if it's just one verse
a day. Meet me in the mindset of approaching
each day with Your armor of protection and
anchor of hope that keep me grounded
no matter what comes.
In Your name I pray.

AMEN.

GOD WILL REPAY

Do not avenge yourselves; instead,
leave room for God's wrath, because it is
written, Vengeance belongs to me;
I will repay, says the Lord.

ROMANS 12:19

Father, it is so very hard not to strike back
at someone who has wronged me. Give me
wisdom to know the line between standing
up for myself and walking away to leave
justice in Your hands. I trust in You during
the good times, I will trust in You during the
difficult ones as well. I rest in knowing You
keep Your promises in Your time.
I lift my heart in praise.

AMEN.

DON'T BE FOOLED

Satan disguises himself as an angel of light.
II CORINTHIANS 11:14

Lord, there are so many counterfeits to
capture a child's attention and heart.
Satan is so crafty at looking appealing and
good. I need discernment for recognizing
his attempts at working his way into my
home—and I need wisdom for getting him
out. Please guard and protect us with
Your presence and light.
In Your mighty name I pray.
AMEN.

HIS WAY, HIS TIME

The Israelites set out whenever the cloud was taken up from the tabernacle throughout all the stages of their journey. If the cloud was not taken up, they did not set out until the day it was taken up.

EXODUS 40:36-37

Father, I want my own way. My mind plans and plots and prepares to carry out my own dreams in my own logical thinking. Help me to stop! I want to stop trusting in myself and start seeking wisdom for Your direction and Your timing. I have made enough messes getting ahead of You or falling behind. I want to be in sync with the way You have planned for my journey in life. I lift my eyes toward You today.

AMEN.

BETTER THAN GOLD

*Get wisdom—how much better it is than
gold! And get understanding—it is
preferable to silver.*

PROVERBS 16:16

Father, I want more of Your wisdom
for each day. You are Creator, Savior,
Redeemer. You are the Alpha and the
Omega. You are omniscient, omnipotent,
omnipresent. And You are good. You are
the very essence of wisdom, so why would
I not want more of You? Help my life to
reflect my devotion to a wholly devoted
God so others will want more of You too.
I love You.

AMEN.

NOVEMBER

GRATITUDE

GRATEFUL FOR
NEW SEASONS

*May [Joseph's] land be blessed by the
LORD ... with the bountiful harvest from the
sun and the abundant yield of the seasons.*
DEUTERONOMY 33:13-14

Father, fall brings a cool, windy breeze
and change of landscape that carries
excitement and nostalgia to my spirit.
It's a lovely reprieve from the hot and dry
summer season. You do the same for my
heart and life: even though fiery trials
prevail, I have the constant hope of rest and
refreshment and for new ways to see Your
majesty and glory. I am grateful for and abide
in knowing I can count on Your faithfulness at
every turn in life's seasons.
All praise be to You.
AMEN.

HIS LIGHT
OF LOVE

When darkness overtakes him, light will
come bursting in. He is kind and merciful.
PSALM 112:4 TLB

Lord, this time of year generates extra
blackness and extended hours to the night
sky. But I see this as lovely because of the
extra beautiful backdrop it makes for Your
stars and galaxies to shine. The numerous
constellations, the planets and their
moons—they all radiate the beauty of
Your creation as a gift of mercy and
forgiveness You bring to a sinful world.
I'm so grateful for the light of hope You
bring and the reminder of Your constant
and faithful love to me.
In Jesus' name.
AMEN.

COLOR IN WINTER

Every good and perfect gift is from above,
coming down from the Father of lights,
who does not change.

JAMES 1:17

Father, help me relay to my child the beauty
in evergreen trees and how they portray
Your presence. When all other trees have
lost their leaves to the grip of approaching
winter, evergreens remain the same—
glowing with life. They are reminders of
Your constant provision for our needs,
both spiritual and emotional. No matter
how bleak the season we're in, Your
goodness, Your blessing, Your love, and
Your Spirit remain the same. Because of
this, we will not be shaken. We will endure.
And we will not lose hope.

AMEN.

GRATEFUL FOR THE AROMAS OF LIFE

To God we are the fragrance of Christ...
an aroma of life leading to life.

II CORINTHIANS 2:15-16

Lord, fall smells are all around—
from bonfires crackling, pot roasts
simmering, apple pies baking... They are a
delight to the senses and a comfort to take
in. I can't help but think of Your provision
and goodness to my family and how, in
turn, I want to be a pleasing aroma—
a fragrance of Christ—that keeps us bound
together. Help me create a haven at home
where Your Spirit of peace and
goodwill lingers throughout.
In Your sweet name.

AMEN.

REST IN HIS CARE

For you who fear My name [with awe-filled reverence] the sun of righteousness will rise with healing in its wings. And you will go forward and leap [joyfully] like calves [released] from the stall.

MALACHI 4:2 AMP

Father, the cooler weather and falling of leaves bring a simple, childlike joy to my heart. It's a season to retreat from the heat of summer trials and rest in Your cool, healing touch. My spirit wants to run and jump with abandon into Your arms the way I'd jump into fresh piles of leaves. I know You'd catch me and that I'd rest carefree while gazing up at Your goodness. I'm grateful to have such a sweet and loving Lord.

AMEN.

REFLECTING ON HIS GOODNESS

I remember the days of old;
I meditate on all You have done;
I reflect on the work of Your hands.

PSALM 143:5

Father, the shortening of days and
crispness in the air make me want to enjoy
Your goodness in the simple things—
like squirrels gathering acorns, fires
crackling in fireplaces, geese honking and
flying overhead. I love sharing them with
my family. I love to talk about past fall
memories and make new ones we can talk
about the next year. Your abundance is all
around, and my heart is full.
I am truly thankful.

AMEN.

SEEKING HIS FACE

*He will receive blessing from the LORD,
and righteousness from the God of his
salvation. Such is the generation of those
who inquire of Him, who seek the face
of the God of Jacob.*

PSALM 24:5-6

Father, as I anticipate seeing friends and
family during the upcoming holidays,
I pause because some gatherings will be
joyous, others more stressful. But in them
all, I want to seek You. Not just when we're
alone together, but I want to be close with
You through every situation I find myself in.
Ultimately, I want to see You face-to-face
now and for all of eternity.
Until that time comes, I seek You.

AMEN.

GRATEFUL FOR HIS PROTECTION

Trust in Him at all times, you people;
pour out your hearts before Him.
God is our refuge.

PSALM 62:8

Father, just as my home provides refuge
from the harmful elements outside,
You are a refuge and place to rest my heart.
I am grateful for Your protection and for
always being a place of warmth and peace
to run to. And just as I decorate my home
to reflect this season, I am adorned by Your
grace and loving care in the seasons of
my soul. You are my safe haven.
All praise and glory to You.

AMEN.

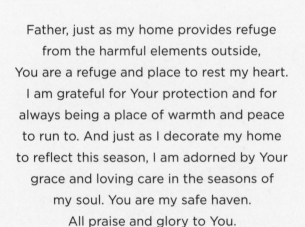

GRATEFUL FOR
LAYERS OF LOVE

*He has clothed me with the garments
of salvation and wrapped me
in a robe of righteousness.*

ISAIAH 61:10

Lord, as the weather gets cooler,
I'm beginning to layer my clothes,
wear a fall coat, and wrap my neck with
a scarf. This reminds me of how You clothe
me with Your saving grace and wrap me in
Your redeeming love. You are a garment of
salvation for my soul, and You protect me
from the harsh elements of this world.
I am so grateful for Your care, and I'll
carry this reminder in my heart today.

AMEN.

GRATEFUL FOR HIS FULLNESS

I have told you these things so that
My joy and delight may be in you,
and that your joy may be made full
and complete and overflowing.

JOHN 15:11 AMP

Lord, this cooler weather calls for a steaming hot cup of cocoa, coffee, or tea. Just thinking about it brings happiness and comfort to my thoughts and mood. Even though I have some challenges to face, filling my mug makes gratitude rise in my heart for the joy You bring into my life. I am filled to the brim with Your simple goodness and pleasure, and I am grateful.

AMEN.

GRATEFUL
FOR GROWTH

So let [your patience] grow, and don't try
to squirm out of your problems. For when
your patience is finally in full bloom, then
you will be ready for anything, strong in
character, full and complete.

JAMES 1:4 TLB

Father, I am grateful for growth. I'm the
same height on the outside, but, compared
to a year ago, I'm taller on the inside.
It's not been easy, but You've stretched and
grown my character, my patience, my faith,
and my trust to new levels. What used to
shatter my nerves no longer has the power
to rob me of the peace that You give.
And I've discovered I find greater joy
as I seek what brings You joy.
All praise to You.

AMEN.

GRATEFUL FOR HIS NEVER-ENDING LOVE

Neither death nor life...nor things present nor things to come, nor powers, nor height nor depth, nor any other created thing will be able to separate us from the love of God.

ROMANS 8:38-39

Father, I see it in relationships all the time: when trials come and days get difficult, someone leaves. It's hard not to feel sad, especially this time of year when family and friends are supposed to gather, not split apart. But one thing brings solace: You will never leave. You promised. There is nothing we can do to turn away Your presence and Your love. You are here to stay no matter what. I love You, Lord.

AMEN.

GRATEFUL HE IS FOR ME

The LORD your God is going with you!
He will fight for you against your enemies,
and He will give you victory!
DEUTERONOMY 20:4 NLT

Father, I'm grateful You are for me—
You fight daily on my behalf. At my beck
and call, You swoop in to guard and protect
me from the things I can see, and You
constantly battle in the realms I cannot
see. You hear my inner cries for help and
ignite a supernatural power and strength to
see me through every day. Thank You for
winning the battles I face and giving
me perfect peace in You.

AMEN.

GRATEFUL FOR MY CHURCH FAMILY

*After [Paul and Barnabas] arrived
and gathered the church together,
they reported everything God had done
with them and that He had opened the
door of faith to the Gentiles.*

ACTS 14:27

Lord, how I love gathering together with
others and sharing about Your faithfulness
and love. My backyard is a safe haven for my
family to meet other believers and to give
and receive much-needed encouragement.
I am so grateful to have such a place to
gather, a place where we don't have to have
our lives together, because we rarely do!
We come as we are, and I know that Your
love and healing await. Your presence is a
wonderful gift, and I thank You.

AMEN.

GRATEFUL FOR HIS OMNISCIENCE

God is greater than our hearts,
and He knows all things.

I JOHN 3:20

Lord, I'm glad You know all things.
I'm glad You know my heart better than I
do. I'm glad You know how problems will
turn out and that You hold my future in
Your hands. I'm glad You are in control and
that You have more love than will ever fit
into my heart. I'm glad You are my God and
that You do not change. I'm glad to know I'll
be with You forever. Jesus, I am glad.
In Your sweet name I pray.

AMEN.

GRATEFUL HE CHEERS ME ON

Anxiety in a person's heart weighs it down,
but a good word cheers it up.

PROVERBS 12:25

Father, just as I cheer on my favorite
football team or a child's performance in
a band concert or school play, I know You
are cheering me on for building my faith
and living with integrity. I know because
You lighten my spirit and bring me great joy
with each whisper of love You speak into
my life. So the next time I feel anxious, help
me to stop and listen and receive the notes
of gladness You have waiting just for me.
You know just what to say,
exactly when I need to hear it.
You are so good, and I love You.

AMEN.

GRATEFUL HE MEETS ALL MY NEEDS

Your Father knows the things you
need before you ask Him.

MATTHEW 6:8

Lord, when I think back on all the times
You've provided for my needs, I feel bad
that I don't trust You more with my future.
Why do I worry when You've been nothing
but beyond faithful to me? Please forgive
my anxious thoughts and help me to rest in
complete surrender to Your ways and Your
power and Your plan for meeting my needs
now and in the days ahead.
In Jesus' name.
AMEN.

HIS WORD
ABOVE
ALL OTHERS

The Son is the radiance of God's glory
and the exact expression of His nature,
sustaining all things by His powerful word.

HEBREWS 1:3

Lord, it's so easy to get confused by conflicting stories in the news; it's hard to listen with much heart and focus. He said, she said, and all is said with anger and hate. It's hard to find anything that is sound and genuine and shared in love. I'm so grateful I can turn to Your Word and be brought to a place of quiet and peace. Your Word is true, and I can rest on that alone. Your Word sustains all things, therefore I can stand secure and not waver amid the confusion. Thank You for being a steady force of truth.

AMEN.

GRATEFUL HE
KEEPS US SECURE

We have this hope as an anchor
for the soul, firm and secure.

HEBREWS 6:19

Father, there are hurricanes, flash floods,
snowstorms, and high winds swirling around
the globe forcing people to evacuate homes
and flee for their very lives. This makes me
think of the times my circumstances flurry
out of control and create unstable ground
in which to rest my soul. But You, Lord, are
steady and secure—You guard and keep
me and my family safe from giving in to a
hopeless tomorrow. You are my strong tower
and keep me anchored and fortified to live
in confidence and with courage.
And I am grateful.
In Your great name.

AMEN.

GRATEFUL FOR HIS ABUNDANCE

Now to Him who is able to do above and beyond all that we ask or think according to the power that works in us...

EPHESIANS 3:20

Lord, this past year has had many challenges, but as Thanksgiving approaches, I can't help but think about Your abundance in my life. You haven't just answered prayer and given blessings, You've shown up beyond measure. You've been faithful beyond what I even dreamed to ask or think. But that is Your way—You are mighty in all that You do, and You do everything to perfection. You will not be matched. My heart sings a song of praise and thanksgiving.

AMEN.

GRATEFUL FOR THE LITTLE CHILDREN

Let the little children come to Me, and don't stop them, because the kingdom of God belongs to such as these.

LUKE 18:16

Jesus, I am grateful for each colored handprint and drawing hanging on my refrigerator door. They bring pure and innocent life into my home. The lopsided flowers drawn off-center outlast and outshine every bouquet on my table. The uneven heart shapes remind me that every heart is beautiful when it beats for You. A child's colorful mind poured out creates simple and beautiful masterpieces. They are a sweet glimpse of why You love children. And I love them too.

Thank You, Jesus.

AMEN.

GRATEFUL TO RECONNECT

If then there is any encouragement in Christ... if any fellowship with the Spirit... make my joy complete by thinking the same way, having the same love, united in spirit, intent on one purpose.

PHILIPPIANS 2:1-2

Lord, I am so grateful for family and friends and time to reconnect and tell of Your faithfulness. Sweet stories remind me that You love my family even more than I do. Difficult stories remind me that You are sovereign over all, and in You I place my trust. You watch over us when we're apart, and You reunite us with the bond of love in ways that are precious and priceless. All thanks be to You.

AMEN.

GRATEFUL FOR
HIS GOODNESS

You ascended to the heights.... He causes
the springs to gush into the valleys.
PSALM 68:18, 104:10

Lord, I'm grateful for the joy of cooking
and baking, fellowship and football.
Each family dish carries stories of the
past—a walk through "remember when"
that brings nostalgic memories to life.
The touchdown roars and fumble gasps
remind me of my mountaintop moments
and valley falls. You've been with me in
them all, and You'll be with me in
the ones to come.
Thank You for being a great, great God.
AMEN.

PERSISTENT IN HIS LOVE

Do not lack diligence in zeal;
be fervent in the Spirit; serve the Lord.
Rejoice in hope; be patient in affliction;
be persistent in prayer.
ROMANS 12:11–12

Lord, I am grateful for Your all-encompassing provision, faithfulness, loving-kindness, and hope. Give me the courage, tenacity, and determination never to give up, no matter how hard circumstances may get. Help me to be a shining example for my children and the next generation to keep the torchlight of Your love glowing until You call me home.
AMEN.

GRATEFUL FOR OUR ANCESTORS

*Teach [My commands] to your children,
talking about them when you sit in your
house and when you walk along the road,
when you lie down and when you get up.*

DEUTERONOMY 11:19

Father, thinking back on my ancestors
makes my heart swell with gratitude—
for their courage, bravery, and endurance.
Most of all I'm thankful for the belief and
trust they showed and for not giving up
hope. I am proud to carry on their tradition
of celebrating their faith. They gave thanks
and acknowledgment to You, and it's a
tradition I want to carry on as well. You are
wonderful to provide such abundance both
then and now. All praise to You.

AMEN.

GRATEFUL FOR REST

*[Jesus] said to [the apostles],
"Come away by yourselves to a remote
place and rest for a while."*

MARK 6:31

Father, I am grateful for after-dinner
strolls that lead to oversized-chair naps.
The slower pace, the rest You give my
soul in this busy life is a respite I need and
receive to the fullest measure possible.
This time affords me space to rejuvenate
my body and fill my mind with quiet and
peace. You bring the deepest calm and
sleep to a very busy season. Thank You for
time to rest in Your presence, Lord.

AMEN.

MEANING IN
THE COLORS

Every good and perfect gift is from above,
coming down from the Father of lights, who
does not change like shifting shadows.

JAMES 1:17

Father, I normally don't like pulling out
tangled Christmas lights to hang on the
house, but this year I consider the colors of
Your light in my life: red for the blood You
shed for me; blue for the healing power of
Your Word; green for the new life You have
brought and still bring each day; white for
Your pure and Holy Spirit; and purple for
Your royal robe of sovereignty, wisdom,
and devotion. Put them together, and
they are a splendid diadem to behold
the majesty of Your throne.
You alone are worthy of praise.

AMEN.

GRATEFUL FOR ME

You knit me together in my
mother's womb.... I have been
remarkably and wondrously made.

PSALM 139:13-14

Father, I am grateful that, as Your creation,
I can be totally me. That in Your eyes and
in Your care, I don't have to put on airs or
be anything other than who You've made
me to be. This is so freeing, and I'm relieved
that the only purpose I'm to fulfill is the one
You made me for. No matter how the world
says I should live, I am safe and confident in
Your plan for my life. Thank You for giving
me space and being a place where I can
let down all masks and walls
and know I am loved.

AMEN.

PASSING THE TORCH

In every situation [no matter what the circumstances] be thankful and continually give thanks to God; for this is the will of God for you in Christ Jesus.

I THESSALONIANS 5:18 AMP

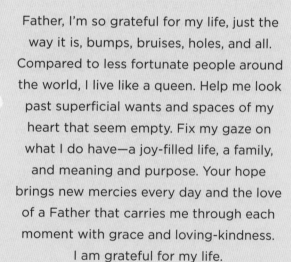

Father, I'm so grateful for my life, just the way it is, bumps, bruises, holes, and all. Compared to less fortunate people around the world, I live like a queen. Help me look past superficial wants and spaces of my heart that seem empty. Fix my gaze on what I do have—a joy-filled life, a family, and meaning and purpose. Your hope brings new mercies every day and the love of a Father that carries me through each moment with grace and loving-kindness. I am grateful for my life.

AMEN.

GOD'S NATURE CAN BE MINE

Give thanks to the LORD, for He is good.
His faithful love endures forever.

PSALM 136:1

Father, I am filled with more gratitude
than I know how to express for Your
eternal nature. Your love, Your hope,
Your faithfulness, Your mercies—they are
all eternal promises that stand true forever.
They are a garland to wear around my
neck and claim as my own. I am humbled
knowing Your very essence resides in me.
You are breath, You are life, and I
worship You with all my heart.
In Jesus' name.

AMEN.

DECEMBER

WHAT REALLY MATTERS

SOAK IN THE WONDER

Come and see the wonders of God;
His acts for humanity are awe-inspiring.
PSALM 66:5

Father, as I face the days and weeks leading
up to Jesus' birthday, remind me to pause
at times to simply soak in the wonderment
of the season: the sights, the lights,
the sounds, and the aromas... Give me
the same anticipation Mary and Joseph felt
as they approached Jesus' birth so
the miracle of that day remains at the
forefront of my mind and heart.
In Jesus' precious name.
AMEN.

KEEP IT SLOW AND SIMPLE

Remember the wondrous works
He has done, all His marvelous works,
and the justice He declared.
PSALM 105:5 CEB

Lord, I confess I feel anxious about the approaching season because of all the distractions that call for my time, attention, and money. They're diversions that point away from You instead of to the miracle of Your birth. Help me not to get swept up in the trappings of materialism, overspending, and overindulging. Help me to pace myself for a more simplistic and meaningful celebration of Your birth, especially with my children. I don't want any of us to miss the true reason for this wonderful time of year.

AMEN.

BE FILLED
WITH COMPASSION

When [Jesus] saw the crowds, He felt sorry
for them because they were hurting and
helpless, like sheep without a shepherd.

MATTHEW 9:36 NCV

Father, I know that the Christmas season
is often the most difficult for many people.
Help me to be sensitive to everyone I
meet. Help me to really look into people's
lives, have compassion on them, and show
empathy wherever it's needed. I want
to be the love of Jesus to broken hearts
and extend kindness to those who need a
helping hand. Help me to be a light of
joy who just might turn someone's
difficult day into one that is blessed.
Glory to You in the highest.

AMEN.

COME TO THE QUIET

Faithful love and truth will join together;
righteousness and peace will embrace.
PSALM 85:10

Father, please take me away to a quiet
place today even if only in my mind.
The noise and the bustle all around make
it hard to be still and reflective of Your
majesty. I want to absorb the magic of
Advent season and what it means to this
world and to me and my family. Keep me in
a full awareness of Your presence so I can
share it with others I meet today.
In Jesus' name.
AMEN.

A HUMBLE HEART

Be like-minded and sympathetic,
love one another, and be compassionate
and humble...giving a blessing,
since you were called for this,
so that you may inherit a blessing.

I PETER 3:8-9

Father, Christ was the ultimate example of
humility. He had to humble Himself to come
down to earth, be born in a manger,
live as a human being, and die on a cross.
Please give me a humble heart, too, to be
ready to act and to serve as Your Spirit
leads. I want to be a gracious touch in
someone else's day today, planting and
spreading seeds of Your love wherever I go.
All glory to Jesus.

AMEN.

BE A BLESSING

Remember the words of the Lord Jesus that He Himself said, "It is more blessed to give than to receive."

ACTS 20:35 NET

Lord, shopping for gifts is fun, but it can also be a breeding ground for getting caught up in commercialism and going into debt. Guide me, Lord, as I navigate this giving season. Where would You like me to spend my money, time, and effort? Help me teach my children that sometimes giving a listening ear can often mean more to others than things. Show us a clear path to who, when, and where to shine Your light and not miss out on any opportunities that You bring. In the spirit of Your love.

AMEN.

BURST FORTH IN SONG

My lips will shout for joy when I sing praise to You because You have redeemed me.

PSALM 71:23

Lord, the carols from years past and
present capture my heart of love for You.
Your joy is made complete in me when I
sing out words telling of Your arrival and
the gift of salvation You are to a lost world.
I want my life to be a song of joy for You.
You are my King and Savior, and I lift
my voice in worship and praise.
Joy to the world through You.

AMEN.

CLOTHED IN RIGHTEOUSNESS

My soul, bless the Lord! Lord my God,
You are very great; You are clothed
with majesty and splendor.

PSALM 104:1

Lord, I pray for my children to truly
experience the excitement of Your birth,
Your presence, Your wonder, and Your love.
With all the choir rehearsals, school and
church plays, I pray that their hearts are
warmed and blessed by the reality of it all.
Help me to keep steering their thoughts
more toward what this season is about and
less toward the hype and glitter. I want Your
majesty and splendor to shine above all else
in their hearts. In Your majestic name I pray.

AMEN.

TAKE TIME
TO REFLECT

Our LORD, I will remember the things You
have done, Your miracles of long ago.
PSALM 77:11 CEV

Jesus, I want to think and reflect on nothing
but You right now—what Your birth meant
to the world over two thousand years ago,
and the significance it still carries today.
You came to save us. You came to show us
what love is. You came to speak truth and
bring grace and show us the glory of God.
You came to die so that I would live. Jesus,
I want to carry the beauty of Your essence
in my heart today as I meditate on the day
You came—the day of Your amazing birth.
Hallelujah.
AMEN.

THOUGHTFUL GIVING

Peace I leave with you. My peace I give to
you. I do not give to you as the world gives.
JOHN 14:27

Father, there is so much unrest in this
world today, so much distraction toward
things that don't matter in light of eternity.
Help me to have Your peace in spite of all
the commotion and busy schedules.
Help me to walk in Your peace as I interact
with my family and others I meet. I want
Your peace to spread as a steady and
bright light in what can often be a stressful
time for many. Let there be peace.
Let there be more of You.
AMEN.

LET YOUR HEART SING

Sing a new song to the Lord!
Sing it everywhere around the world!
PSALM 96:1 TLB

I sing praise to You today, Lord!
I ascribe to You the glory due Your name,
and I worship You in the splendor of Your
holiness. Your mighty works and wonders
are marvelous; they are too numerous
to count. May my life be a song to You
today, my actions a sweet melody, and my
thoughts a pleasing aroma.
This is a wonderful time of year as I
count down the days until Your birth was
announced by the angels. I thank You for
this time and this moment to relish the
wonderful gift that You are.
AMEN.

REMEMBER HIS WORKS

I will also make every effort so that
you are able to recall these things
at any time after my departure.

II PETER 1:15

Father, I'm so grateful for family traditions.
They remind me of Your faithfulness as well
as preserve memories for us to grow on.
My heart smiles from memories of friend
and family time together, as well as Your
blessings to us over the years. Yes, there
have been struggles, but You have been
faithful through them all. I'm filled with
so much hope for the future, which fuels
my desire to keep serving You without
wavering, no matter what. You are so good.

AMEN.

HOPE AMID
THE MESS

Be strong and let your heart show strength,
all you who wait for Yahweh.

PSALM 31:24 LEB

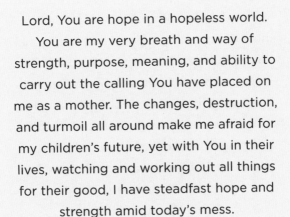

Lord, You are hope in a hopeless world.
You are my very breath and way of
strength, purpose, meaning, and ability to
carry out the calling You have placed on
me as a mother. The changes, destruction,
and turmoil all around make me afraid for
my children's future, yet with You in their
lives, watching and working out all things
for their good, I have steadfast hope and
strength amid today's mess.
All glory to You.

AMEN.

HE IS JOY
TO THE WORLD

In Your presence is fullness of joy.
PSALM 16:11 AMP

Lord, before knowing You, I didn't
know the meaning of joy. I had occasional
happiness, but true joy runs so much
deeper. You have graced my life and my
heart with the ability to be in the heights
no matter what is in my depths. It is a gift in
a world that constantly tries to take
joy away. But because of You, I have joy
to the fullest, and I am grateful.
Thank You for loving me.
AMEN.

A TASTE
OF HEAVEN

*The bread of God is the One who
comes down from heaven and
gives life to the world.*

JOHN 6:33

Jesus, Your birth, Your life, Your death,
and what they mean to this world are
literally a piece of heaven on this earth.
You, Your goodness, Your pure and holy
love are a foretaste of what is to come in the
future. The essence of heaven flows through
my every heartbeat. Even when I get busy
and don't acknowledge it—it's always there.
Thank You for coming down.
Thank You for saving me.
Thank You for saving the world.

AMEN.

BEAUTY IN OBEDIENCE

"I am the Lord's servant," said Mary.
"May it be done to me
according to your word."
LUKE 1:38

Father, I can only imagine being in Mary's
place of trusting You with an immaculate
conception. Her obedience and grace are
an amazing example of following You,
going where You lead, and doing as You
say when nothing around makes sense.
I draw strength from her story. Help me to
be like that. Help me to believe with all my
heart that You have a plan for my life and
for my child's life—a greater plan than I
could ever dream. I trust in You.

AMEN.

LIGHT OF
THE WORLD

*I am the light of the world. Anyone who
follows Me will never walk in the darkness
but will have the light of life.*

JOHN 8:12

Jesus, how very dark this world, and my
life, would be without Your light to shine
through. I pray my children will see the gift
of Your light as well. I want them to know,
without a doubt, that You are with them,
lighting the way for them to go. Help us all
to reflect Your light onto others this season,
to draw in and gather hearts that are
hungry for hope and longing for healing.
All praise and glory to You.

AMEN.

BREAD OF LIFE

"I am the bread of life," Jesus told them.
"No one who comes to Me
will ever be hungry."

JOHN 6:35

Father, as I enjoy all the treats and
special meals with friends and family,
make me mindful of the sustenance You
provide when I cling to You. Help me not
indulge in things that won't fulfill beyond
the present moment but rather take You in
for lasting pleasure and satisfaction.
Fill each and every void so that cravings
for the world disappear to where all I
have and want is more of You.
I hold You close to my heart.
AMEN.

HE LOVED FIRST

See what great love the Father has given us
that we should be called God's children.

I JOHN 3:1

Lord, Your love compares to no other.
You came down to save me before I
even believed in or cared about You.
Your love came first and wooed me in
with an embrace I couldn't resist. Your love
covers my sins, past and future, and makes
me Your own. Your love increases my love
for my family, even on days when they
aren't so easy to love. My heart is Yours
because nothing equals or comes close
to what Your love has done for me...
for all of us.
Thank You, Jesus.
AMEN.

UNITY FOR
THE NATIONS

Most of all, let love guide your life,
for then the whole church will stay
together in perfect harmony.
COLOSSIANS 3:14 TLB

Lord, just as You came to bring unity
among the Jews and the Gentiles, may
we have unity among the nations now.
I pray for peace to one day rule over
the fighting and destruction that are so
prevalent. May that peace begin with me—
to strengthen my family's bond, to be a
constant example that keeps us together,
and to extend Your love to sisters and
brothers in our church body
and community.
To You be all the glory.
AMEN.

HE IS KING

[God] is the blessed and only Sovereign,
the King of kings, and the Lord of lords.
I TIMOTHY 6:15

Father, to think that the Spirit of the
King of kings and Lord of lords lives in me,
in all who believe in You, is a miracle.
Your very nature resides in us, which makes
me pause and give great thanks. I worship
and adore You for the gift of Jesus' birth
and the power of His sovereignty. He is
Heaven Come Down, and I bow down to
His majesty and preeminence in my life.
Hallelujah.
AMEN.

HE SEEKS OUT
THOSE HE LOVES

*The Son of Man has come to seek
and to save the lost.*

LUKE 19:10

Lord, You not only came to save the lost
in this world, You came to seek them out—
first. You actively looked for and sought out
me, a sheep that was as lost as lost can be.
And Your pursuit of love is relentless to this
day. Your grace abounds in every wrong
thought, rebellious act, and self-centered
agenda. And You make it clear that Your
love is faithful—nothing can separate me
from it. Who is anyone to deserve such a
love? You alone are worthy to be praised.

AMEN.

HEALING IN
HIS WINGS

For you who fear My name, the sun of
righteousness will rise with healing in its
wings, and you will go out and playfully
jump like calves from the stall.

MALACHI 4:2

Jesus, the only births I can honestly celebrate
are the births of each of my children. They were
so special to me, yet I know that their births don't
compare to Yours. Your appearing, Your Spirit
are all evidence of the supremacy of love and a
healing balm to a depraved world.

You give life to places once dead, and hope
to hearts that used to be empty and without
purpose. No other occasion compares to that
of Your coming to earth. This world longed for
something or Someone to hope in, and You
fulfilled that longing. All my joyful praise to You.

AMEN.

ABIDE IN
HIS PEACE

For a child will be born for us.... He will be
named Wonderful Counselor, Mighty God,
Eternal Father, Prince of Peace.

ISAIAH 9:6

Lord Jesus, with painful and chaotic
times in this world, I'm grateful to have
Your peace to hold on to. No matter what
my circumstances try to dictate, I am not
alone to face them. I can literally rest in
Your presence knowing that whatever my
surroundings look like on the outside,
You will remain a steadfast anchor of calm
on the inside. My challenges may be great,
but You are greater and over them all.
Thanks be to God for Your peace.

AMEN.

IMMANUEL—
GOD WITH US

She gave birth to her firstborn son,
and she wrapped Him tightly in cloth
and laid Him in a manger.

LUKE 2:7

O God, glory to You in the highest!
I celebrate Your arrival in the depths of
my heart. Thank You for coming down,
for living among us, for sharing the glory of
the Father, and for covering me with Your
grace. Your life gives my life new meaning.
I pray for the new life my family has
through You as well. We all have purpose
for today and hope for the future. You are
the greatest gift this world has known,
and I embrace You with abandon.
Praise and honor and glory to You.

AMEN.

PROCLAIM
HIS COMING

The angel said to [the shepherds], "Don't be afraid, for look, I proclaim to you good news of great joy that will be for all the people: Today in the city of David a Savior was born for you, who is the Messiah, the Lord."

LUKE 2:10-11

Father, thank You for sending Your Son, Jesus! And thank You for the gift of my children. Thank You for the wisdom, the teaching, the promises that are ours through Him. Thank You for providing a way for all of us who believe to have eternal life with You. Help me to pass my belief and faith in You onto the generations to come. In Jesus' great name I pray.

AMEN.

CHOOSE TO FOLLOW HIM

Behold, the star, which [the Magi] had seen in the east, went on before them [continually leading the way] until it came and stood over the place where the young Child was.

MATTHEW 2:9 AMP

Father, as the wise men followed the star to

where Jesus was born, I follow Your shining light of love with all sincerity and passion. You lead in the way of refreshing truth, and Your presence of joy pierces my heart with immeasurable effect. There is none like You. You are the Savior of the world, and You are my friend who only wants the very best for me today and for eternity. I love You and thank You for coming to this earth. Glory in the highest.

AMEN.

MEDITATE ON
HIS PRESENCE

*Mary was treasuring up all these things
in her heart and meditating on them.*

LUKE 2:19

Father, let me never get so caught up in the

hurriedness of life that I forget to pause and
dwell on Your goodness. I love being still
and meditating on what You have done for
the world and what You have done for me.
Jesus is a miracle of redemption and saving
grace in countless ways. I am so grateful
and honored beyond the depths to be
called righteous, a saint, and the least bit
good. It's only because of Your nature in
me that this is possible.
Bless Your holy name.

AMEN.

OUR GREAT REDEEMER

*[Anna] came up and began to thank
God and to speak about [Jesus] to
all who were looking forward to
the redemption of Jerusalem.*

LUKE 2:38

Jesus, thank You for being a God of
second, third, and numerous chances in life.
Thank You for taking time and talent I've
wasted and redeeming it for Your glory now
and in the future. Thank You for turning
what the enemy has meant for harm into
a life story that reveals Your power and
goodness. May I never be silent but always
speak about Your presence in my life, giving
You all the glory. You alone are worthy.

AMEN.

SOVEREIGN OVER ALL

Proclaim the LORD's greatness with me;
let us exalt His name together.

PSALM 34:3

Father, I praise Your name and Your greatness. You are the One true God, and I believe that You are and will remain sovereign over all. You are absolute in a world that is wasting away. You are supreme over all that has ever existed, including my life. It humbles me to know that You love me, and yet You do. I exalt Your name and give You all praise and honor. Glory to You in the highest.

AMEN.

THANKSGIVING FOR ANOTHER YEAR

Only goodness and faithful love will pursue me all the days of my life, and I will dwell in the house of the LORD as long as I live.

PSALM 23:6

Lord, thank You for another year of life and growth, lessons learned, and wisdom gained. As I look back, I see Your loving-kindness and gentle mercies stamped all over my days, and I feel grateful. Even with the trials, I am glad. I am richer in love because I know You more. You have been faithful in the past, and now I pray for Your faithfulness in the new year to come.

In Jesus' great name I pray.

AMEN.

DaySpring

LIVE YOUR FAITH

Dear Friend,

This book was prayerfully crafted with you, the reader, in mind—every word, every sentence, every page—was thoughtfully written, designed, and packaged to encourage you...right where you are this very moment. At DaySpring, our vision is to see every person experience the life-changing message of God's love. So, as we worked through rough drafts, design changes, edits, and details, we prayed for you to deeply experience His unfailing love, indescribable peace, and pure joy. It is our sincere hope that through these Truth-filled pages your heart will be blessed, knowing that God cares about you—your desires and disappointments, your challenges and dreams.

He knows. He cares. He loves you unconditionally.

BLESSINGS!
THE DAYSPRING BOOK TEAM

Additional copies of this book and
other DaySpring titles can be purchased
at fine bookstores everywhere.
Order online at <u>dayspring.com</u>
or
by phone at 1-877-751-4347